Meaning, Mattering, Transcendence

Meaning, Mattering, Transcendence

Essays on Meaning, Morality, and God

Vernon White

CASCADE *Books* • Eugene, Oregon

MEANING, MATTERING, TRANSCENDENCE
Essays on Meaning, Morality, and God

Cascade Books
An Imprint of Wipf and Stock Publishers
199 W. 8th Ave., Suite 3
Eugene, OR 97401

www.wipfandstock.com

PAPERBACK ISBN: 978-1-6667-6486-4
HARDCOVER ISBN: 978-1-6667-6487-1
EBOOK ISBN: 978-1-6667-6488-8

Cataloguing-in-Publication data:

Names: White, Vernon, author.

Title: Meaning, mattering, transcendence : essays on meaning, morality,
and God / Vernon White.

Description: Eugene, OR : Cascade Books, 2023 | Includes bibliographi-
cal references and index.

Identifiers: ISBN 978-1-6667-6486-4 (paperback) | ISBN 978-1-6667-
6487-1 (hardcover) | ISBN 978-1-6667-6488-8 (ebook)

Subjects: LCSH: Philosophical theology. | Language and languages—
Religious aspects.

Classification: BL41 .W55 2023 (print) | BL41 .W55 (ebook)

06/21/23

Contents

Introduction

Musing on Meaning

What does it all mean? A good question. . . . Nobody knows what anything is; a man can only learn what a thing means

GEORGE MACDONALD, *LILITH*

THERE IS NO SHORTAGE of pressing issues to engage the intellect in these early decades of the twenty-first century. Our natural, social, political, religious, and intellectual worlds are all stressed and struggling. We face an age of anxiety with little or no sign of any new (or old) ideological or pragmatic program to rally us. Most of these issues take concrete form. The natural world is burning, flooded, poisoned. Social and political life is fracturing into competing identities. Truth is being twisted to support particular political ends. These things matter, and rightly rise to the top of our agenda. So what provokes me to write instead about more abstract and metaphysical issues? Why muse about *meaning*?

It may help to explain the exact nature of what I want to pursue. What concerns me in particular is the way basic moral and religious terms are so often referred to in public commentary without examined meaning. Terms like "right," "good," "God," are common currency in both confessional and secular contexts, but their meaning slides past our scrutiny even though crucial to the

1

argument or narrative. A discussion whether a moral course of action should trump expedience depends entirely on what we really mean by "moral." A discussion whether God exists depends hugely on what we really mean by "God." Yet outside specialist academic discourse these terms are rarely examined. We may assume we have a shared world of meaning when we use these terms. But how do we know—unless we are prepared to investigate?

In particular there are the unexamined assumptions about a distinct, *sui generis* meaning in such terms. Moral language is almost invariably used in this way. It almost always carries an implicit claim to uniqueness. "I did it because it was the right thing to do" suggests reasons for action which are distinctly moral, not just pragmatic or utilitarian, however closely these overlap. "She was a good person" suggests a distinct moral evaluation, not just an estimation of her talents, achievements, or personal attractiveness. Religious language likewise. "God" normally refers to a unique kind of reality distinct from other realities in the world, however closely connected with them. If God is replaced with the general term "transcendence" much the same applies. The transcendence of profound spiritual, aesthetic, or relational experiences seems to refer to a unique experience radically beyond the normal limits of ordinary life, however deeply embedded in it.

This assumption of uniqueness may well be justified. But it surely needs investigating, not just asserting. Otherwise it offers a major hostage to fortune, all too easily inviting just a reductionist riposte. To understand terms purely by their difference from everything else risks saying nothing. It begs the question about their positive meaning. What do "rightness" or "goodness" or "God" mean positively? Do they actually mean anything? Or are they just a refuge for nonsense? Do they simply act as a cover for the absence of *any* credible meaning? Herein lies the reason why these abstract questions about meaning deserve attention. Properly examined they touch on why and whether some of the most basic foundations of meaning are credible at all. Put another way, it is a process of reflection about why anything at all really *matters.*

It is a potentially risky business. Pursuing these questions can lead in very different directions. On the one hand Occam's razor comes readily to hand. Reductionism is not just the easy riposte but an entirely possible outcome of serious thought. We can quite plausibly think our way to the view that morality and God do not mean anything distinctive at all. Both may well be seen *just* as social and psychological constructs. Morality may be just pragmatism, God just a personal or tribal projection. Instead of convincing us, the claim to unique meaning may only raise the even more radical question of what we mean by meaning itself. What is meaning anyway? What do we mean by the meaning of anything? *Is* there any meaning to a meaning which is not just a human or social construct?

On the other hand this is certainly not the only outcome possible. With reflection we may equally become persuaded that reductionism does not convince. As I shall argue, it may seem to offer an implausibly thin view of reality. Although morality and God are hard to define in themselves they still gesture to *some* sort of unique category of thought and experience which cannot be dismissed. They refer to realities which uniquely illuminate the rest of life even though elusive in themselves. To be sure, this needs to be established. It cannot simply be asserted, any more than reductionism. But then that is exactly why these issues have to be faced as honestly as possible.

This is nothing like new ground which I'm proposing to cover. Analytical moral philosophy and philosophical theology have long pursued these questions in academia. They offer close and rigorous analysis of meaning in a variety of contexts. But this is often technically expressed, highly specialized, and hard to access. What I want to do here is explore these questions in a more accessible, less specialist, inter-disciplinary way. I also unashamedly want to argue a particular case in the process. I hope to recover some confidence that there *is* meaning to be found in the current shifting sands of social and intellectual unrest. Moral language is not endlessly slippery or redundant, nor is religious faith. Even more important, meaning itself is not just a chimera. Things *matter*.

It remains a largely abstract pursuit. This collection of essays does not, on the whole, directly address those specific concrete issues which are so insistently making their claim on us. At best this quest for meaning will help establish their general seriousness, but does not often suggest any very particular or practical response. Nor is it the only way of pursuing meaning. Those of us saddled with a persistently reflective cast of mind have to accept that the meaning we crave is just as likely to emerge from active participation in life as from reflective thought. Rather like happiness, meaning often appears in the pursuit of something else, discovered more often as an accident than as a goal. If we intentionally try to chase it down in its own terms it is fickle. Pay it too much attention and it can blur and recede, rather than clarify and grow. The sense of it may disappear altogether.

Nonetheless, one way or another the chief point remains. Meaning matters. The issue is not put to bed just because it is elusive or (apparently) abstract. We do not become indifferent to meaning just because we cannot or will not easily pin it down. In fact, like the air we breathe or the love we long for, meaning actually matters more when it seems to elude our grasp. Any sense it just might not be there at all is even more disconcerting and provoking. If meaning disappears altogether, human life is so eviscerated the fear of its absence is likely to make us grasp at it more not less. In other words, although the presence of meaning can be enjoyed without much thought, its absence cannot. In its absence it craves more attention. It provokes a pursuit as a matter of urgency, not just as a matter of intellectual curiosity. It suggests an *a priori* status to meaning, as if it is a kind of presupposition of being human at all—which of course a moment's reflection confirms. After all, how could we continue to function honestly at all in any of our personal relationships or projects without confidence in some sense of meaning? How could we assume any purposiveness, accountability, or responsibility?

All this is why some musing on meaning seems unavoidable, whatever the limits of abstract reflection. And it is why I now offer this short collection of essays, which ponder meaning both in itself and in relation to fundamental issues of existence and belief. They offer reflections on the meaning of meaning, meanings of morality, and meanings of God. And in each case they are driven by exactly this instinct that the unexamined meaning of important things we do, say, and believe, is not always secure, so trying to examining it matters. They are driven by this conviction that it is a matter of integrity at least to try.

What sort of essays are they? They are freestanding. All except the first have some origin in self-contained lectures, talks, or articles, suitably revised and refreshed. But equally they also have a clear connection and a deliberate order. The connection lies in a common trajectory towards what I call "ultimacy" or "transcendence." To muse on the meaning of meaning always pushes us to some ultimate ground of meaning beyond, as well as within, ourselves. To wonder at the meaning of morality leads in a similar direction, to a notion of ultimate value beyond as well as within our own selves. To reflect on meanings of God is the attempt to give some sort of content to this ultimacy and transcendence.

These connections between the ultimacy of meaning, morality and God, are not presented as logically compelling. They appeal to a sense of congruence, resonance, fittingness, not rational necessity. Nonetheless the intuitive links are there. They are the reason why meaning, morality and God are all more persuasive when taken together rather than unravelled. I do not claim they *must* belong to each other, but I do believe they fit well. This also applies to their order, which is similarly presented here more intuitively than logically or theo-logically. Traditionally the logic of metaphysics and theology has begun with God, from which morality and meaning derive. Here I have reversed this order simply to reflect what I take to be the more complex and varied phenomenology of our actual experience. In the experiential world, meaning emerges variously according to context, and we are just as likely to move from meaning to morality to God as the reverse.

What all this amounts to is not a comprehensive or systematic treatment. These are essays, bite-sized commentaries, no more. They touch on big general issues of metaphysics and morals, but do not engage with all their consequences nor all their wider hinterland. They take soundings from Western moral philosophy, literary study, theology, but do not draw on other global traditions. They offer fresh connections from within a large field of enquiry, but they do not claim an original scholarly contribution in any one area. They aim to offer a concise, original, and distinctive pathway through much existing scholarship (and ordinary human experience), not to plough a fundamentally new furrow. I offer some referencing for academic specialists but, as indicated, I avoid too much technical discussion for the sake of the more general reader. In short, they have very clear limits.

Nonetheless my hope is that the insights and connections offered like this will prove fertile, in a different way to the traditional academic monograph. The intention is to be accessible without being superficial, to engage with a wide spectrum of readers. The philosophically and theologically minded reader of faith may be most naturally at home in some of it, but it is also written for the non-religious and post-religious reader. They are reflections for anyone who is teased, tormented, frustrated, by a failure to examine the meaning of these terms right, wrong, God, and the transcendent. Above all, they address this most basic of all questions. *Is* there any credible and distinctive meaning in our existence, in morality, and in God? I believe these questions will always matter, whatever the state of the world we inhabit.

"Le Sens du Sens"

The Meaning of Meaning

BELIEVING THAT THERE IS meaning in life is part of the human condition. It is a basic human need, not just a religious dogma. Most of us live most of the time on the assumption that things, events, experiences have meaning. But this is not universal or incontrovertible. Life can also appear meaningless. This may be simply a matter of bleak, raw, experience. Or it may be a more considered reflection on experience. We can *decide* there is no meaning. We can believe meaning is an illusion. Like the imagined meaning of the mystery echo in Forster's *A Passage to India*, it registers, but we are skeptical about it. We conclude there is nothing there. The transient and fickle nature of our actual experiences of meaning and the apparent randomness of events reinforce the skepticism—is *all* meaning only a chimera?

Questions of Meaning

In asking this question, however, we are also raising a prior set of even more basic questions. What is meaning? Is meaning the same as "mattering," another way of describing the varied and problematic significance of things and events? If not, how do they correlate? What do we *mean* by meaning? What is "le sens du sens?"[1] What do we mean specifically by perceptual, not just linguistic, meaning? What is it that we are perceiving when we experience meaning? When we experience meaning are we just encountering a construct of our own mind and experience (or other people's minds and experience)? Or does meaning have an objective grounding beyond it as well? Are we simply acknowledging a psychological phenomenon, an emotional "charge" which we attach to some things or events? Or are we perceiving some other quality in things which claims us regardless of our own state of mind? Other questions follow. Is it possible anyway to ask questions about meaning as a generic term? Since there are many radically different kinds of meaning—moral, aesthetic, factual, semiotic, relational, logical and more—can meaning per se be considered at all, or only particular meanings?[2]

There are unlikely to be straightforward answers to these questions. It is not an easy terrain to explore. It may seem anyway a futile and irredeemably abstract exercise. Yet it remains the case that we live largely on this assumption that there *is* meaning, or meanings. Meaning, by definition, real or imagined, engages us constantly. So should we not at least try to understand more about it?

One semantic issue could be resolved straightaway simply by stipulative definition. "Mattering" is sometimes used interchangeably with meaning. But in fact I suggest mattering functions more often in ordinary speech as both a quantitative and qualitative qualifier to meaning, not just as a synonym. In other words what matters is meaning which is particularly intense or important in some way. This will depend on context. Logical and mathematical meaning, for instance, may matter hugely in some contexts (in a

1. Cf. Ferry, *Man Made God.*

2. Wittgenstein famously defined linguistic meaning by its use. But he was more ambivalent about proposing any theory or understanding of the meaning of meaning itself. Cf. Conant and Sunday, *Wittgenstein on Philosophy*, ch. 10.

computer program monitoring a patient's heartbeat) but hardly at all in others (solving an equation just for intellectual satisfaction, like doing a crossword for fun). In short, what matters is simply what is *significant* meaning in a given context.

But more substantive issues are not so easily resolved. Most critically, there is this underlying issue of objectivity. The question of whether and how anything objective underwrites meaning, or whether meaning is purely subjective, is clearly both core and problematic. The problematic arises because while the *prima facie* presentation of meaning in experience is undoubtedly subjective, this does not exhaust the experience. Our experience of meaning also presses us towards objective accounts. But how then should we understand this objectivity? This, surely, is the place to begin, so what follows attempts to unwrap this issue first—if not to resolve it at least to help understand it better.

Subjectivity and Objectivity

The subjectivity in meaning, first, is evident. It lies obviously in the simple fact that, by definition, all our experience is subjectively mediated. This in turn may easily suggest (more radically) that meaning is also subjectively generated, not just subjectively mediated. This is partly a function of its apparent transience, its fickleness and fluidity. What any event, experience, object, relationship means to you or me, and how much it matters, so often appears entirely contingent, dependent on the vagaries of our circumstance, temperament, personality, background, past experience, culture. It can change radically and with disconcerting rapidity, individually and collectively. The trivial can at one moment assume gargantuan proportions of meaning, then recede only a few hour later. Sometimes this seems due just to the passage of time. Who has not experienced the bewildering change of perspective (about almost everything!) just between 3:00 a.m. and 8:00 a.m.? At other times it is precipitated by a new event. Who, adult as well as child, has not had obsessive concern about one issue—a spot on the skin, a scratch on a toy—which is wholly displaced by something else altogether—a family fall-out, an illness, a job promotion? What once mattered now becomes trivial. In other words, our individual perception of meaning is endlessly transfigured. Collectively it is much the same. Many social and cultural concerns also turn out to be passing fashions, transient as mist on a cold window pane. They seem to matter at the time, then no longer. Think of manners, dress, some gender issues.

The point is, all this fluidity naturally fits with an entirely subjective source. It easily suggests that meanings have no stable or objective reality of their own beyond our own mind. They are just our own creation, individually and collectively. So various disciplines explore this territory just in these terms. Psychologists, neurologists, psychotherapists, anthropologists, sociologists, linguists, philosophers, all consider why one thing matters to us more than another, why some sorts of mattering change, and usually assume this instability arises precisely because it is a subjective domain being explored. They are exploring a sphere of creation and interpretation in the human mind.

To be sure, these disciplines may also refer to more objective socio-biological and evolutionary aspects. If something works in an evolutionary sense it acquires and retains meaning as long as it functions in this way, and this implies at least a kind of (instrumental) objective basis to shifting meaning. Even so, the subjective interpretation of meaning retains its priority, not least because there is no easy correlation between intensity of meaning and any instrumental usefulness. The subjective intensity of mattering we experience in a particular event does not always match any objective evolutionary value it may have. The beauty of a setting sun can stir the soul profoundly with hardly any evident survival function. The same is true of other objective realities which might seem to provide a basis for meaning, whether of fact or value. They do not provide a reliable guide to the intensity of what matters to us subjectively. Neither the empirical facts of science nor the moral demands of society will always correlate with our subjective sense of mattering. They frequently fail to engage our attention at all. The most intense sense of meaning is more likely to be found in human relationships and personal ambitions, and these can generate meaning with almost no regard at all for objective criteria of survival, social morality, or any other external norm. All this points to the capaciousness of the subjective domain of meaning, and to its dominance. It might well also suggest it is its sole source.

Yet there remains this paradox. For all its capacity and variety, does an exclusively subjective realm of meaning *wholly* satisfy? Surely not. Does there not also remain, for most of us, a profound sense of meaning in some notions of truth and morality regardless of any subjective feelings we have or do not have about them? Most obviously, acts of injustice or altruism, and statements of truth or falsehood, have this depth of meaning. Even when they fail to engage us subjectively they still register with significance. Does it not still matter profoundly, for example, if a child (or anyone) suffers appallingly, whether or not we are much moved subjectively? Does it not matter that truths of physics shape reality, whether or not we personally care about them or understand them? Of course it does!

In other words, meaning measured only by what a psychotherapist has aptly described as its subjective "emotional charge" simply does not exhaust meaning. Far from it. Meaning which is *only* subjectively conceived and affectively received can actually appear superficial, capricious, arbitrary, compared to these other kinds of deeper meaning. We might even say it becomes relatively meaningless. In that sense a purely subjective account of meaning subverts itself and leads inexorably back to objectivity. Some element of objectivity still seems to be required. In fact it becomes irresistible. It functions as a bulwark against this general regression to meaninglessness within purely subjective meanings of meaning. It helps account for this peculiar kind of depth with which some things seem to "really" matter regardless of our subjective engagement. To affirm this objective element to meaning, as well as its evident subjectivity, therefore seems vital.

Of course this does not settle all questions. How can any objective basis to meaning be understood? Where does it come from? How does our subjective perceptions of things relate to these objective truths—moral or factual? And if there can be no simple binary reduction to either subjective or objective definition, how else can we refer to meaning? In short, meaning remains elusive, beguiling, complex. Perhaps this is why it is often better displayed than argued or analyzed. It is why meaning is most often explored in the domain of art, literature, imagery, fictional narrative, poetry—and most tellingly in the narrative of "real" life, the experiences of a lived life.

However, this does not close down the quest for understanding. It just suggests we should broaden the field of enquiry. It may mean we need to press our questions about meaning through the lens of the arts and lived experience as well as analytical argument. It may also suggest we should try to offer a fuller phenomenology of meaning in its most basic manifestations, to dig deeper as well as wider. But how can this be done?

Conditions or "Sites" of Meaning

One way to advance this sort of enquiry, but retain a manageable focus, is to consider meaning at a more fundamental a priori level. That is, we should press questions about meaning by reviewing the basic conditions under which it emerges, not just in its more developed form. This is not quite the same as simply reviewing the chief sources of meaning. Key sources of meaning such as human relationships, moral experience, aesthetic experience, are fertile ground for discussion, but they are already highly interpreted experiences of a specific kind. Likewise with semiology, the study of signs. Linguistic and other signs are rich sources of meaning, but as communicative events they too are already interpretative acts of a specific kind. By contrast, conditions of meaning are prior to all these, even though they overlap. They refer to those basic structures of reality (including human reality) which allow *any* kind of meaning to emerge. They will be the sites where our experience appears intrinsically and pre-cognitively organized or shaped to produce this impact we call "meaning."

By interrogating these we should surely approach more closely meaning itself, and five of them now follow. They are not exactly equivalent. Some are more foundational than others. Their order reflects their significance in experience rather than any logical priority, and they interrelate closely in any case. But overall they offer at least some sense of what these conditions might offer.

Meaning from Narrative

One basic condition of meaning most recognized in modernity is the narrative structure of experience. To be sure, this too may already be a specific interpretation of reality. It is also much contested. Postmodernity especially has been deconstructing narrative almost to extinction. But not quite. Some *form* of narrative (whatever its content) still haunts, and re-inhabits, even these deconstructions.[3] In that sense there is still a case to be made for narrative generally as a fundamental and pervasive condition of meaning. Narrative of some sort remains a core site.

But what is the basic form of narrative meaning? It is not necessarily just linear and goal-based. There are other ways of linking events to convey meaning. Nonetheless, there is little doubt that the sense of linear movement towards a goal is one key form, and it is not hard to see why. When we are purposively engaged in projects, meaning is generated precisely by goals being pursued. Within each plan or purpose in which we are engaged, within each role we assume to pursue the goal, actions assume meaning. Both subjectivity and objectivity may be involved in the process. This narrative structure can be conceived either as a projection of the human mind onto reality, or as intrinsic to the grain of reality, or both. But whichever of these is the case, the structure itself is what allows meaning to emerge.

It is equally the case that this narrative form also raises critical questions about the meaning it generates—and this too will be important for any ultimate meaning of meaning. Meaning is questioned by this narrative form particularly by the precarious status of goals themselves. After all, in due course the goals within a narrative

3. Cf. Julian Barnes's deconstructions of narrative in his fictional work: discussed in White, *Purpose and Providence*.

are either attained or discarded, or found to be beyond reach. Either way the project has come to an end. What then of its meaning? Even more de-stabilizing is the final end to narrative which is imposed by our finitude and mortality. Can any narrative meaning or series of meanings remain meaningful in the face of death?[4] In short, alongside the power of purposive narrative to generate meaning it also paradoxically draws attention to its own intrinsic instability.

This, however, only raises precisely this question we are pursuing about ultimate meaning. *Is* there any ultimate meaning of meaning? Is there, in Luc Ferry's terms, any final "sens du sens"? This phrase of Ferry's is mesmerizing, especially in its short, spare, French form, because it seems at one and the same time a circular question and a fertile one. Is meaning ultimately only self-referential, or is there an underlying or generic ground and source of meaning which could connect all the particular finite meanings of all our various projects, even when they end? Does it require a further, wider narrative to secure the meaning of all these finite provisional narratives? Since that in turn might lead only to infinite regress, what would then secure that further narrative?

In short, narrative both generates meaning and presses these questions about itself. And these are ultimately metaphysical questions, only answerable by a view of reality which may include narrative but also transcends it altogether. This will be contested, as is all metaphysics. But it could ground its objectivity better, so surely remains to be considered.

Momentary Meaning

Narrative, however, is by no means the only basic site of meaning. It does not fully capture the texture of life. Some like Galen Strawson even argue that narrative is hardly significant at all in their experience.[5] So it is important to look at other primary sites as well. What, for instance, of the meaning of "moments" where

4. "The question of meaning [*per se*] comes to the fore in the face of finitude." Ferry, *Man Made God*. Italics my addition.

5. See for example Strawson, *Things That Bother Me*, ch. 2.

meaning seems to emerge in disconnected moments rather than from any wider narrative in which the moments are connected and embedded?

This is apparent, for example, in the performance of music, or the experiences of human relationship. These can appear to contain meaning as much in apparently self-contained moments as in their succession. It is, arguably, as powerful and pervasive a dimension of experience as linear narrative meaning. To be sure, there is ambivalence here too, or at least an instability, but again this is potentially fertile. The ambivalence lies in the fact that these apparently disconnected moments still tend to generate meaning by suggesting *some* sort of connection, even if not a straightforward linear or causal connection. These connections may, for example, constitute a "figural" (non-linear) *pattern* in moments and events.[6] And this is fertile because, as with linear narrative, it raises a question about any one particular pattern. Can this sustain meaning in itself, or does it need some further grounding? If so, what is the nature of that underlying basis? Does this too have metaphysical implications?

The distinction between the meaning of narrative and the meaning of a moment could also be mapped in terms of "extrinsic" or "intrinsic" meaning. This distinction can apply both to events and things. On the one hand significance appears to be a relational property that supervenes only because of what happens *around* a particular event or thing. In other words, the meaning of any particular event (or thing) does not inhere in the event itself but depends on what has preceded and what follows it (or what surrounds an object). The meaning of a particular pass in a game of football, for example, depends hugely on the rest of the game. This is its extrinsic source of meaning. On the other hand we can also find meaning in an event (and thing) in its inherent nature, i.e., a property which somehow makes sense of the event or thing in

6. A figural meaning arises in a connection between events where there is no evident causal, linear, or temporal link. Instead it is found atemporally in a familiar resemblance or common pattern between these otherwise unconnected events or moments. See discussion in White, *Purpose and Providence*, 100–102.

itself, and which does not depend on any goal it has yet to achieve, or any other object to which it relates. A particular pass may have self-contained technical brilliance, regardless of its role in the rest of the game. A tree standing in isolation commands attention, whether or not we see its relation to the wider ecology around it. This is its intrinsic source of meaning. It reflects a profound instinct, widely acknowledged and articulated, that life's moment are not to be evaluated just for their fit into an external purpose.[7] They are to be savored for their intrinsic worth. They have their own inner "ends."

Analyzed in this way momentary or intrinsic meaning is therefore characterized more distinctively. But does this then have any further bearing on the meaning of meaning itself? I think it does. One thing to note is the persistence of *purpose* it indicates in meaning. Purpose is most obviously connected with narrative in the fulfilling of goals and pursuing external projects through a sequence of actions. But there is purpose too in this momentary meaning. And that is precisely when we see the purpose contained intrinsically in the event (or thing). It lies in an event being itself, rather than trying to be something else or *for* something else.[8] This is often clearest in particular moral acts or aesthetic experiences, such as an exquisite musical moment. In some accounts of morality and aesthetics, acts and events do not just resonate with a good achieved for the whole or a pleasure given to others, they are also engaging us by their own inner intrinsic moral or musical integrity. This can also be true of natural objects. To consider the deep roots of an oak tree, as Philippa Foot has suggested, is to see that they are not just useful for some external goal (e.g., surviving longer) but part of a purpose built into the very nature of what it is to be an oak tree.[9]

---

7. William James references this instinct, for example, in his influential philosophy of pragmatism.

8. Cf. Affolter, "Human Nature as God's Purpose," 445–50.

9. Foot, *Natural Goodness*. Cited in Affolter, "Human Nature as God's Purpose."

This fact that purpose relates to meaning in momentary as well as narrative form does not itself directly arbitrate on the issue of objectivity. In principle a sense of purpose, internal or external, can still be subjectively projected as well as objectively perceived. But it does add emphasis to purposiveness per se as a core ingredient of meaning. Meaning, it seems, relates closely to purpose whether it emerges from narrative or moments, extrinsically or intrinsically, in events or things. And because purpose needs some grounding, this in turn does again invite metaphysical questions about ultimacy and objectivity, even though not strictly requiring them.

From these first two conditions of meaning, then, at least this much begins to emerge as a picture of what it is. Meaning, it seems, always includes a *purposive* dialectic of both moments and wider narratives. It is also always a restless dialectic, pressing beyond itself for more objective grounding, asking these metaphysical questions about itself, even though not (yet) decisively answering them.

Meaning, Mind, and Transcendence

But what else should we consider when looking for basic sites or conditions of meaning? What for instance about the basic category of mind and consciousness? There is no meaning of any kind without some sort of conscious mind. Both giving and receiving meaning occurs in the operation of our minds in some way. So what might this yield about the meaning of meaning, given further thought?

There are different frames of reference to explore here. In a strictly secular, humanist, anthropocentric context, the experience of giving and receiving meaning is exclusively the preserve of human minds. Meaning comes ultimately from human minds alone. The meaning of things and events arises only when projected by human thought and intention. The inanimate world has no meaning in itself to offer. The stars have no intended meaning for us in themselves. Their meaning supervenes only from our own (or other person's) state of mind when we observe them. If we wonder at them, this arises as a quality we ascribe to them rather than receiving from any mental activity they possess (which would just be an instance of pathetic fallacy).

Within a wider metaphysical frame this interpretation can change. A Gaia-like metaphysics which ascribes mentality to the rest of non-human reality, or a theistic metaphysics which ascribes divine purpose operating within the world, both suggest other possibilities. They allow the possibility that we can receive meaning from the things of the world as well as project it onto them. This makes meaning more extensive and resonates with a great deal of that human experience (with or without religious belief) which claims to find even inanimate reality responsive, not inert. Literary expressions of this sort of meaning can be particularly telling here. Think for example of the novelist and poet Thomas Hardy, skeptical himself but often allowing favored characters like Tess to express this experience on his behalf. Natural processes around her were "part of her own story" we are told, as an explicit statement of what is actually implicit throughout.[10] Philip Pullman likewise frequently describes experiences in which his mind seems to be receiving meaning *from* the world. For Pullman this comes especially through the experience of the connectedness of all things (of which more later). He describes "the sense that the whole universe is alive, not just inanimate but alive and conscious of meaning . . . connected by lines, chains and fields of meaning, and I was part of it."[11] Pullman denies this sense is necessarily mystical, dualistic, or suggestive of any other particular metaphysic. For him it is not evidence, for example, of a separate category of Spirit "behind" or "in" material things. Yet he reports it nonetheless as a profound experience of meaning coming from the world, received and recorded by his own mind.

Whatever the metaphysical frame, however, the wider point here is that meaning does seem to be arising from an intimation of some "other" impinging on our minds (whether another human, the wider world, or divine). In particular the testimony is about *receiving* this meaning from the other, not just projecting it. And

10. Hardy, *Tess of the d'Urbervilles*, 91.
11. Pullman, "God and Dust," 437–38.

this is a critical further aspect of mapping meaning. In the first instance it simply adds to the general sense of some form of objectivity in meaning because meaning is being experienced as sent to us by another. But more than that, by locating this so firmly in the receiving mind, it also nuances the meaning of this objectivity. It is nudging us more to a notion of transcendence rather than pure objectivity, going beyond a merely binary objective-subjective distinction which downgrades the role of the subject in the experience (something strongly resisted by both Hardy and Pullman). It suggests instead a notion of transcendence in which the self is still included in the experience of the other. In fact Pullman resists explicit language of transcendence, but the experience he recounts nonetheless describes it perfectly. It is exactly how he describes the ultimate source of his storytelling: "It feels like the story I'm writing already exists . . . something has come from somewhere else."[12] In other words, what has come to his mind from an other is truly within his mind while also being truly from beyond. Both objective and subjective are present, but indivisibly.

This sense of transcendence is a vital dimension of the ultimate meaning of meaning, the "deep" mattering of meaning. It is evident through words and signs, as well as things, events and experiences. The meaning we receive from all these is both within our mind and *beyond* the conscious thinking in our mind. So, for example, the meaning I receive from other people's words may often resonate with a "surplus" of meaning which goes beyond original intentions or expectations of either giver or receiver (think how a promise or threat can function in a human relationship). It is even more apparent with events and things. The meaning I receive from the birth of a child, a grave illness, the sound of birdsong, the quiddity of mountain range, a moment's eye contact, a successful business transaction, frequently transcends anything I or anyone else is consciously intending or projecting.

In short, the sense of transcendence in the human mind in these contexts seems to tie the meaning of meaning to a reality *both* within *and* beyond any one human mind or intention. So this

12. Pullman, "Poco a Poco," 227–28.

too is what "le sens du sens" must include. Meaning is the open-ended, restless, dialectic of purpose in both moments and narratives. It also arises inextricably in this meeting in our mind of what is both within and beyond itself.

Meaning in Order, Connectedness, Congruity

This last feature of transcendence is apparent in another basic condition of meaning. This is the sense of order and connectedness (or congruence). It is another core site of meaning which is ambivalent, inviting a transcendent reference to help make sense of it. And it is a particular aspect of this general experience of the mind appearing to meet something beyond itself in which it also participates within itself.

The perception of connectedness and congruence between things is particularly formidable in the way it generates meaning so extensively. It arises persistently in so many arenas. It is found through a sense of history, in personal narratives, through encounters with the natural world, and in scientific method and discourse. Of course, the contrary experience of randomness, chaos, fragmentation, is equally formidable. So it is always going to be moot whether order and connectedness represent an objective feature of reality itself or only the mind's projections onto reality. Moreover, since the mind is anyway so embedded in the world it experiences, neither physics nor philosophy is able to arbitrate decisively on this. That is precisely its ambivalence. But then the point here, once again, is that this ambivalence only helps raise the metaphysical question. Since it persists even through its apparent contradictions, does this point to a transcendent ground for it?[13]

Literary expressions are again helpful. They are often the most eloquent expression of this sense of connectedness. The allusions to a sense of connectedness in Hardy and Pullman have already

13. Sociologist Peter Berger memorably described these intuitions of an ultimate order (in spite of so much immediate evidence to the contrary) as "rumours of angels." They are persistent and hard to dismiss. Cf. Berger, *Rumour of Angels*.

trailed this. They illustrate first how widespread this is. It is not the preserve of an explicitly religious worldview (both are skeptical). They also illustrate how profound the experience is. To be sure, when Hardy's Tess (quoted above) was whimsically finding natural events like the weather congruent and connecting with her own story, Hardy's own view is hidden within the fictional character he has created. This is the value of an ironic voice. But elsewhere it is clear how affected he was himself by these perceived patterns and correspondences between things, in spite of his rational skepticism. The great "web" of reality was beloved especially by Victorians, and Hardy was no exception. The sense of an interconnected "network or tissue which quivers in every part" was clearly an eloquent site of meaning both for him and others.[14] Pullman is even more explicit: "I just saw connections between things, similarities, parallels; it was like a rhyme, but instead of sounds rhyming it was meanings that rhymed. . . . The physical world itself was full of meaning. . . . I felt at one with the physical world and I saw what it *meant*, and what it meant was that I belonged in it."[15]

As indicated, Pullman himself does not interpret this as a religious experience with a source in the divine: "I didn't feel at one with God; I felt at one with the physical world." Nonetheless, he is still noting that he finds profound meaning here. The connection *resonates*. Specifically he is finding this meaning in the nature of a world which is connecting both within himself and beyond himself. And that is what makes it an experience of at least some kind of transcendence, whether or not described religiously. It is what makes this sense of order and connectedness yet another ingredient in any ultimate meaning of meaning.

Time

Finally, what of the flow of time itself (I mean time in any form, not just as the locus of narrative and moments)? Isn't this an obvious

---

14. Hardy, diary entry March 1886, cited in Beer, *Darwin's Plots*, 157.
15. Pullman, "God and Dust," 438.

basic condition of meaning as well? Temporality *per se*, whether in its sequences or extracted moments of time or both, is surely necessary to meaning. So what more might this yield?

A similar pattern emerges. Meaning *is* undoubtedly made possible by time. But again it is not secure because time also invariably deconstructs meaning as well facilitating it. It carries the meaning of both moments and narratives, but also compromises them both. This has already been touched on. In relation to moments, time carries us inexorably and serially from one moment to another. That means single moments, however intense and illuminating, are never secure in themselves, they can never be wholly captured or wholly indwelt in time. In relation to narrative, the same flow of time means we only stand in one part of it with limited perspective, the past irretrievable and the future inaccessible, with no complete or secure narrative available. That means narrative meaning can only be perspectival in time, and can never be a true whole.[16] In short, it appears that a *final* meaning of meaning can never be fully grasped in time even though meaning is intrinsic to time. It is another form of the paradox which teases throughout these sites, another example of a condition of meaning both generating and potentially undermining meaning.

Yet precisely in that way, it is again suggestive. For doesn't this too invite a transcendent reference? Specifically it begs the question of eternity, suitably defined. After all, an eternity conceived as a dimension of existence including both moments and narratives, but also transcending them in an eternal whole, would clearly be a resolution. The meaning generated by time would be entirely secured by such a "time-ful" eternity. Such a conception, a form of transcendence which both includes and goes beyond our normal categories of time, becomes, in this context, almost irresistible.

Of course this resolution is not compelled. The paradoxes of time and temporality could be dissolved simply by rejecting any notion of final resolution at all. No ultimate meaning of meaning actually *needs* to be offered in any form. Yet it remains inviting. When meaning so evidently seems to need some relation with

16. Cf. Affolter, "Human Nature as God's Purpose."

temporality, but also so clearly strains beyond it, this sort of "eternalized" temporality cries out to be considered. It is yet another potential dimension to add to the meaning of meaning.

Trajectories of Transcendence

What then emerges overall from these sites of meaning? They offer, I suggest, real possibilities even if not certainties. They take us in a clear direction of travel even if not to a final destination. Something substantive has been harvested from them even if they cannot decisively ground meaning in any one final way. They offer at least some content to the "meaning of meaning," however contested. It is formed and shaped in being, moments and narrative, in which there are both intrinsic and extrinsic dimensions. It is essentially connected with mind, purposiveness, connectedness, and time. And crucially, while it engages us subjectively through its huge emotional charge, it also appears to press on us from beyond ourselves. It at least gestures at both objectivity and transcendence.

These trajectories of transcendence in meaning are particularly hard to ignore. They are persistently suggested and sustained across a wide range of social, moral and aesthetic experience, even in skeptical contexts. Charles Taylor has made just this case very persuasively in his monumental history of ideas.[17] He consistently uncovers a "displaced" notion of transcendence persisting even in our currently more immanent frames of reference of the so-called secular age. Simon Critchley does much the same, reluctantly, in a more focussed essay on the "infinite" trajectories specifically of moral experience.[18] The brief phenomenology of the experience of meaning offered here now reinforces this. Whether in narrative or moments, the analysis has consistently showed how the heavy charge of purposive meaning carried in some moral, aesthetic, spiritual experiences at least suggests this ultimacy. Intuitively, if not logically, it keeps pressing us to accept there "must" be an

17. Taylor, *Secular Age.*
18. Critchley, *Infinitely Demanding.*

ultimate or transcendent ground to its meaning. The sense of the mind receiving as well as projecting meaning, and the sense that meaning strains time into eternity, shows the same pressure. Cumulatively these all push us to ground meaning in something more secure than finite and transient human volition. They strain for a metaphysics of transcendence. This in no way denies the reality of the experience of ultimate meaninglessness as well. But it does suggest that the experience of an ultimate meaning, grounded in transcendence, has at least equal persistence and credibility. And it adds immeasurably to the depth of this final meaning of meaning we think we are encountering.

Could we go further? In the light of this phenomenology could we also claim ultimate meaning actually has logical or experiential priority over ultimate meaninglessness? Can we claim meaningless is always and only parasitic on this prior intuition of ultimate meaning? That is less clear to me. I'm not sure this could ever be demonstrated conclusively. So in that sense belief in the ultimate meaning of meaning may have to remain a decision, an act of metaphysical (or religious) faith. Even so, the phenomenology of experience explored here does at least offer a serious architecture of thought to support that faith.

It has also offered some reminders of how much so-called ordinary lived experience supports it as well. As noted at the outset, we do actually *live* as if meaning has ultimate meaning, and it is very difficult to live without it. Again, this is displayed in literature as much as in analytical thought. It surfaces most tellingly when the intention is actually the opposite, to deny ultimate meaning. That denial is simply so hard to do. In the actual experience of life, meaning resists! Julian Barnes's short gem of a novel, *The Sense of an Ending* is a haunting example. He asks there what meaning there is in any life, when life so often offers no necessary or proven "objective" sense we can grasp. To begin with both the narrative and commentary of the story appear to answer only in the negative. Life does *not* make sense. It offers, for example, no meaning like "reward for merit," or "healing for remorse"—that is not "life's business." Beyond the accumulation of experience and its intrinsic uncertainties, there seems to be nothing, no discernible meaning at all: only "unrest . . . great unrest."[19] The quest for meaning has only shown there is none. But then this question inserts itself, subtly but irresistibly. Why then the unrest? What causes the unrest if not some ghost of meaning supervening after all, from beyond? The question is not resolved. But it is raised.

A similar sort of residual meaning emerges when the question is raised by Derrida in more discursive mode. He interrogates the meaning of our lives (as well as our utterances and texts), in order to "do justice" to life—especially in the face of death. "How do you finally respond to your life and your name?" he asks us (also asking himself, as Judith Butler points out).[20] Again no positive answer is offered. But then here too it also seems that just the pursuit of that question, even when it meets the apparent dead end of annihilation, has still raised the possibility that there *is* an answer. Meaning still *resists*.

Meaning, Mattering, and the Mundane

Finally—what difference might all this make? What difference does it make to acknowledge this wider frame of reference for meaning? For example, does it affect or even answer some of our initial questions: Why does meaning mutate so radically through time, even with trivial matters? Why does what matter to us in any one moment prove so fickle? Why is there sometimes a mismatch between matters to us and what "really" matters? Do these now have any kind of new perspective?

I think they do. For what this wider frame of reference for meaning requires is now clearly something more than explanations given just in physiological, psychological, or sociological terms. It insists that the instability of emotional charge we experience in events might not *just* be due to the chemical, psychological, and social formation of our minds engaging in particular moments or

19. Barnes, *Sense of an Ending*.
20. Butler, "Jacques Derrida."

narratives. Instead, this "fickleness" might also be bearing witness to a realm of mattering which transcends our current psychological state, which is impinging on us in another, deeper way. It raises the possibility that the meaning to us of anything, either trivial or momentous, may be being shaped not just by the contingencies of our particular and immediate moods, moments, narratives but also by this wider transcendent reality or narrative. This is what the trajectories of transcendence within meaning are indicating. They are pointing to a deeper mattering which bears on us even when our limited narrative or momentary experience of meaning does not match it. It accounts for the intuition that some things "really" matter even when they carry little or no current emotional charge of subjective mattering—and *vice-versa*. This is what accounts for many of the inconsistencies of our actual sense of mattering. We may not fully perceive this transcendent "interruption" to our subjective feelings, or believe in it, but it bears on us nonetheless.

This deeper transcendent layer of mattering that we (sometimes) perceive makes another difference as well. It is not just an explanation for the inconsistencies we may feel about what currently matters to us. It is also invaluable for flourishing in life more generally by deepening its seriousness. Whether characterized as moral, aesthetic, personal, spiritual (or more platonically as a unity of all these) their transcendent quality is what uniquely gives this ultimate seriousness to meaning in life. It is what, in Derrida's terms, "does justice" to life. And even when the specific content of this ultimate meaning is opaque, elusive, or partial, just the possibility of its presence still lends life this *sui generis* texture. It means life is always potentially valuable and *interesting*.[21] At worst, all too often, it means it is truly tragic. At best it means it is also infinitely rewarding and more joyful. But it always means it is potentially *worth* something.

---

21. Cf. Karl Barth's description of the texture of life lived with a sense of objective (in this case divine) purpose: "Life in the world, with all its joys and sorrows and contemplation and activity will always be . . . a really interesting matter . . . an adventure." Barth, *Church Dogmatics* III/3, 242–43.

Does any more practical outcome flow from this sort of perception? Yes. The distinctive disposition and cast of mind which is shaped by this perception of ultimate meaning will *motivate*, morally and spiritually. It affects how we live in the world, not just how we see the world. How does it do this? On the one hand it keeps us paying attention to things, events, people, even when we feel indifferent to them. Just the possibility they might ultimately matter in a wider narrative than we feel currently engaged with must enlarge our moral, aesthetic, spiritual appreciation of them. It will take us beyond the remit of our current moods or present narrative, draw us out from ourselves, and pull us towards wider horizons for moral and personal responsibility. At the same time, this motivation to pay attention is not oppressive. It is liberating. For unlike a life lived with a solely immanent source of meaning, accepting a transcendent source of meaning releases us from the burden of always having to create and sustain all this meaning ourselves. So it is not overwhelming or paralysing. It is a disposition in which moral motivation and aesthetic appreciation is both enjoined *and* enabled. It offers a kind of grace.

In short, accepting this depth in the meaning of meaning offers a response to life which is constructive, positive, wholly engaged; but also graced. This is surely preferable to a life shaped by meaninglessness or solipsism. It would be recognized by much of the best of religion. It coheres particularly well with the ideals of a Christian religious disposition. But it would also be more widely recognized than that. It doesn't require explicit religious faith to function. And that, most of all, is what this argument has tried to show throughout. This sort of meaning, and this sort of life, arises out of an age-old quest and question of *homo sapiens*, not just of *homo religiosus*. The question was simply this. Can we—without importing (at least consciously) too much specific prior metaphysical or religious freight—find any real "sens du sens"? I think we can.

Meanings of Morality

Two things fill the mind with ever new and increasing admiration and awe, the more often and steadily we reflect upon them: the starry heavens above me and the moral law within me.

IMMANUEL KANT, *CRITIQUE OF PRACTICAL REASON*

KANT'S LAPIDARY COMMENT RESONATES. It still finds a ready echo in modern minds. It is not necessary to grasp or agree with his wider philosophy to connect with this insight that moral intuition evokes wonder. It has a uniquely compelling quality. Whether experienced as law or life, within or without us, an encounter with a moral claim or moral act can be extraordinarily moving.

But what is it? What does it mean to say something is moral? I am not primarily asking here about how we discern what is good and evil, right and wrong (i.e., whether we use intuition, tradition, utilitarian calculus, character, or indeed Kant's own "universalizability" principle). I am asking about what we mean by moral reality per se. It is widely believed to "exist" in the sense that most agree that there will always be some things necessarily described as "right" and "wrong," "good" and "evil." Our disagreements about *what* is moral in particular circumstances do not, on the whole, weaken this core belief *that* morality exists. But what does it mean?

What is it that is being expressed by using specifically moral language? There is no shortage of discussion and contention about this in the discourse of specialist academic moral philosophy.[1] But I now want to convey some sense of it without recourse to highly technical language, if it can be done.

Unique Moral Meaning and Reductionism

Typically we use moral categories to express a *sui generis* (i.e., wholly unique) quality of both attitude and behaviour. This *sense* of distinctiveness persists in our discourse even where morality is formally conceived only as an instance of something else, e.g., as a disguised sense of some non-moral social or evolutionary driver. Even when deconstructed in this way, some attitudes or behaviours continue to present themselves in experience with a distinctive character that demands a distinctive language which we call "moral." It is describing a uniquely authoritative, compelling, absolute, qualitatively distinct kind of claim on us. Usually, though not always, it also presents as an objective claim. Above all, it is felt to be highly significant. Few would describe moral reality just as a trivial or random fact of human psychology or biology, like a taste for chocolate or an occasional headache. Moral discourse is almost always used as if it *matters*, and matters uniquely. Those who are genuinely amoral, without any distinctive sense at all of right and wrong, or its mattering, represent a rare pathology.

This *prima facie* force of distinctive moral experience does not settle all questions about its actual distinctiveness. Reductionist accounts of morality remain plausible. Social necessity, biological mechanisms for survival, the pursuit of pleasure, can always be enlisted to show why moral reality might not be what it seems. They can easily suggest why its apparently distinctive character is deceptive. They offer mechanisms to explain how

---

1. There are "non-naturalists and naturalists, moral realists and anti-realists, cognitivists and non-cognitivists, deontologists and consequentialists, reason-based moralists and desire-based moralists" . . . and more. The range of options is "dizzying." Mane, "Nice and the Good."

non-moral drivers can produce a sense which purports to have unique character, authority, and significance but actually derives wholly from its non-moral sources. Altruism, self-sacrifice, generosity, cooperation, can all be accounted for, after a fashion, by this kind of non-moral explanation. Yet these accounts still have to reckon with the fact that the distinctive moral *sense* persists even after being theoretically "seen through" in this reductive way. It still exercises its unique claim, pervasive authority, and sense of significance, even after a reductionist re-interpretation. There are other reasons as well to dispute reductionist accounts, which I will mention in due course, but it is this enduring *prima facie* character of distinctive moral experience which remains the most powerful riposte. It just will not easily disappear—and so it needs to be addressed seriously as it appears.

Addressing moral experience in this phenomenological way, I need to repeat, does not bypass the theoretical and critical questions of reductionism. They remain unavoidable. Its compelling nature might still be a purely psychological phenomenon rather than a witness to something beyond ourselves. Its sense of authority and absoluteness might still derive purely socially, rather than from some further metaphysics. So the point is certainly not to sidestep these issues. It is simply to approach them by paying attention to the nature of moral experience itself, not just by a priori theoretical argument. This, I suggest, will help uncover its full meaning, and in a more rounded way. It will connect more readily with our actual experience. It will also bear more directly on positive issues of practical living. What does this *prima facie* nature of moral sense mean for human aspiration? What does its ideal character and authority mean for our motivations?

To be sure, this does not mean that any of these sorts of questions need to be asked for us to be morally serious people. George Eliot's fictional characters offer useful exemplars for this. There are characters who felt no great need to explore the ultimate meaning of moral experience in any terms. The absoluteness of the moral demand and its ideals did not impress on them as an issue to be resolved metaphysically because their moral concerns and commitments were not primarily religious or metaphysical but empirical and pragmatic. Yet there is no question of their seriousness about moral realities or their stern sense of moral duty. This duty was fulfilled simply by trying to do what is practically possible rather than resolving the metaphysical implications of an ideal. The temper of this is memorably expressed in the celebrated final reflections in Eliot's *Middlemarch*. Describing the heroine Dorothea, Eliot writes: "[the] determining acts of her life were not ideally beautiful," yet they still resulted in "fine issues." In other words, the moral sense for Eliot here is not just about heroic acts which aspire to meet some absolute metaphysical or divine ideal, but simply aspires for what is possible and will at least make things "better than they would otherwise have been."[2]

This is a perfectly serious response to the moral sense, and it may be tempting to settle for it. Why can't we de-mystify the demands of the moral sense from all metaphysical freight? Why can't we accept it simply as a given ingredient of experience which helps us flourish in practical ways, rather than as a problematic authority needing explanation? We could. It is especially tempting for the naturally pragmatic Anglo-Saxon temperament.

Nonetheless, while this may satisfy some it leaves others unpersuaded. The distinctive authority of morality, for many, needs justification. That is what makes others want to dig deeper and look further, and it is why I now want to reflect more on it. After all, if on reflection the notion of morality really does lead us beyond pragmatism to metaphysics and to faith, it will gain even more significance. Its unique meaning will have a unique mattering, an even greater authority. And many of the key features of morality do lead in just this direction.

Prima Facie Features of Moral Sense

These basic features of moral sense have already been trailed. But they deserve further attention in a more systematic way. This

2. Eliot, *Middlemarch*, 896.

cannot be an exhaustive discussion of them, nor a complete list. Nor will they be presented in order of logical priority, only in terms of experiential significance. There will also inevitably be some overlap between them. Nonetheless, taken together, this should still offer a deeper analysis of moral sense. It will do some real justice to both its texture and "weight" in our experience—and especially to those features which tend to generate these wider metaphysical questions which press on us.

Distinctive, Irreducible

First there is this simple fact that the moral sense presents itself as distinctive and irreducible. As already indicated, it is possible to conceive it otherwise, just as a product of social or natural exigences, a pragmatic need to cooperate, only a disguised outcrop of evolutionary needs. But I have suggested this fails to persuade because its *prima facie* distinctiveness is so pervasive and powerful. It cannot be so easily dismissed. What I also want to suggest now is that there is a weakness in the reductionist argument in itself.

The problem with it lies, as so often, in the word "just" ("just" an evolutionary product). This betrays the slippery nature of the argument and exposes its main flaw. It is the flaw of the genetic fallacy. This is the error of thinking we know the nature of the outcome of a process just from the nature of the process which produced it. Here the error is assuming that because evolutionary processes cause this outcome of a moral impulse, the moral sense is itself only a disguised survival or expediency instinct. This simply does not follow. It is like saying that because the biological means of conceiving a child do not in themselves require thought, feeling, or love, the outcome itself (the child) can have no real capacity for thought, feeling, love. These are only disguised forms of biological processes. This is nonsense. A child has personal capacities even if some processes producing it were impersonal. In the same way the meaning of the moral impulse can be distinctively moral even if the socio-biological processes producing it were amoral.

This fact that our moral impulse really is distinctive is most apparent in moral extremes. To encounter something utterly evil, like the gratuitous hurting of vulnerable young people or the monstrosities of terrorist cruelties, is to be repelled with a weight of feeling which requires distinct categories and language. We do not see these sorts of acts as just inexpedient or impractical, but precisely as *wrong* or *evil*. It is similar when we encounter heroic goodness. Faced with a radically good Christlike life, whether lived in the public gaze or anonymously in the self-sacrificing lives of unknown carers, we are moved and attracted in a distinctive way. We do not see this just as a disguised form of expediency or social contract but as qualitatively different. What we see is magnificently *good*, not just expedient.

This perception of a distinctive and irreducible moral reality therefore remains potent. It cannot easily be dispensed with. And it is suggestive. It provokes questions. Where does such distinctive meaning come from? How can we account for it? If it is not explained in other terms, is it self-explanatory? Or does it require something else to make sense of it? What might this suggest about the nature of wider reality? *Pace* Eliot, these potentially metaphysical questions will keep pressing. So what might they mean?

Objective

Moral reality is suggestive in a similar way also because it presents itself objectively. Objectivity bears different meanings. It could, for instance, simply mean that the sense of a moral dimension is so widespread it cannot be just my (subjective) interpretation. It is a shared interpretation, with a measure of inter-subjective endorsement. That lends it at least an appearance of objectivity.

But this is hardly adequate to the actual experience of moral reality, which goes much further. The rightness of some actions and the goodness of some people or states of affairs (or conversely their wrongness and evil) do not present just as a shared interpretation simply like a shared taste. They present as a description of something which is the case regardless of our judgement about it, even a collective judgement. Inflicting gratuitous pain and betrayal has a wrongness about it irrespective of whether it is deemed wrong by a few or by many. Altruistic care and sacrificial love has a goodness about it regardless of how many of us do or do not view it that way. In this sense the meaning of rightness and wrongness seems to inhere in some kinds of actions or states of affairs objectively in a different and more radical sense. It describes both an analytical and quasi-empirical truth. It is an objectivity like the roundness of a circle and the movement of trees in the wind.

To assert this is partly the expression of an intuition. It is how the meaning of rightness and wrongness present themselves intuitively, especially in concrete situations where much is at stake. But it also has to do with the rational form of the language we characteristically use about moral issues. A sense of objectivity in moral reality is why we characteristically try to offer reasons for moral judgement, in a way we do not for matters of mere taste. When we offer reasons for moral judgement we are trying to show how particular actions or states of affairs conform, or fail to conform, to an objective meaning which might be agreed or disagreed with by others. This is why I can properly be called on to say *why* I dislike racism in a way I am not called on to say why I prefer wine to beer. I simply like wine better, but I do not simply dislike racism—I dislike it for moral reasons.

As with its distinctiveness, this sense of objectivity can be deconstructed. It could be re-presented just as a social construction, in a similar way to its irreducibility. But again, beware the potential genetic fallacy hidden with the "just." What may always be socially mediated may not always be (just) socially constructed. The sense of objectivity may just as plausibly be a reflection of reality as a projection onto it or creation of it. So objectivity too remains a potent feature of the moral sense. And it poses similar, metaphysically freighted questions. If it is not just a social or psychological creation of our subjectivity, what is its ultimate origin? Where does it fit in any wider worldview we may hold?

Authoritative, Binding, Obligatory

Another telling feature of moral reality, already trailed, is the sense of authority it conveys. The moral sense presents itself as a claim which seems uniquely binding and obligatory. We may be free to ignore or reject it, but what we choose to ignore still has weight and significance. It exerts pressure on us which expects a response, even if it does not coerce it. In this respect it is like pain or beauty. It carries within itself a call to react in some way, even if it does not determine exactly how we respond. This sense of obligation to react suggests a law-like quality to moral experience, but it is more personal than the notion of law per se. The claim is more like an encounter with a strong personal will, as though someone rather than something is exerting this pressure of obligation. But whether personal or impersonal, we cannot just remain indifferent. It is making a *claim* on us which is intrinsic to the experience itself, and which registers regardless of whether or how we choose to react.

A simple analogy helps convey the nature of this. Consider our instinctive reaction to crisis or threat which overwhelms us. We cannot normally remain indifferent. We will experience the threat as an immediate trigger for self-preservation, a reaction to a claim on us which is intrinsic to the nature of the unfolding experience. In this context this is not in itself a moral reaction (nor necessarily immoral). But now consider our reaction when the threat is overwhelming someone else, where the moral register is more apparent. Its form is just the same. If we have a moral sense at all there will be no neutral way of experiencing this either. Someone else's dire need will also be experienced as a pressure or claim on us intrinsic to the experience. The claim will be to act in some way to help, or just to sympathize if we cannot act. Although we can refuse (just as, theoretically, we might not act in self-preservation in our own crisis), the one thing we cannot do is experience the situation indifferently.

This authoritative and personal pressure on us, and within us, is often referred to as conscience. But that does not explain, only describes, the experience. This "conscience" with its binding sense of claim will always beg for further explanation. Yes, we may sometime suppose we are only reacting to the force of social demands which we have internalized. But more often the experience of it suggests something beyond merely social constructs. Its authority appears too absolute to be subsumed just under the notion of shifting social mores. In other words, this too will press some to seek a metaphysical (or religious) origin. At the very least it again raises the question.

Energetic, Irrepressible

A further feature, begging similar questions, is the persisting energy of the moral sense. Moral energy is extraordinarily irrepressible. It occurs across all time and space, and in diverse cultures. I do not refer here just to the notable resurgence of moral energy in authoritarian or fundamentalist cultures where there is strict uniformity about what is right and wrong. There is also huge moral energy in liberal societies where there is disagreement and diversity in beliefs about what is right and wrong. Here too we never lose the sense *that* there is a right and wrong and this matters, even when we cannot always agree *what* is right and wrong. In fact, far from discrediting the moral impulse, a diversity of moral ideas often increases moral energy. The moral energy displayed (albeit in ugly fashion) in the so-called culture wars of developed societies is a case in point.

A telling demonstration of how basic moral energy persists even in liberal societies with large areas of moral relativism is the way diversity displaces moral energy into new areas rather than diluting it. Rather than being dissipated by relativism, moral energy re-appears in a new guise. It issues, for instance, in the extreme attachments to identity which have burgeoned in recent decades. It has also issued in the quest for efficiency and accountability. It is notable for example how mistakes of inefficiency or negligence made at work or in public life elicit reactions which are just as searing as if it was malice. Why? It is because these reactions to inefficiency have a displaced moral energy behind them. Put simply, if a culture of relativism means I am no longer sure what is morally right or wrong about sexual ethics or a just war, I attach my moral energy instead to lambasting a hapless call center operator for the inefficiencies of their company. It is, incidentally, this displacement which has helped spawn both the litigious society and the bureaucratic society. But the chief point here is simply to show how irrepressible our underlying moral energy is. And it invites the same questions. If it is so ineradicable, just what is it? Where does it come from?

Perfectionist, Infinite, Absolute

A final, closely related feature of the moral impulse lies in perfectionism, its drive to transcend limits, the absoluteness of its ideals. Atheist political philosopher Simon Critchley, amongst others, notably describes moral sense in this way.[3] Although naturally wary of religion and metaphysics, he nonetheless finds in the moral impulse exactly this "transcendent" drive which goes beyond normal limits. In that sense it has a quality of infinity. He describes it in much the same way as Martin Luther described the unique authority of conscience. Its push and pull is so absolute that it never seems satisfied. In his own words it endlessly "vivisects" us, cuts ever deeper, never satisfied that it has perfect embodiment in us. It would not do this, he says, if it was just the pull of pragmatism; it does so as only as a distinct category of *moral* perfection.

To help make this concrete, think for example of the dynamics of an encounter with someone who falls in the street in front of us. A homeless person, perhaps. What we may experience is not just a limited contractual or reciprocal moral claim on us. It is potentially limitless. Yes, superficially the claim seems limited (help him to his feet if you can) and implicitly contractual (someone might do the same for us one day). But in fact the claim often presents itself more compellingly than that. Should I also check whether there is anyone to look after her? Take him to the hospital?

3. Cf. Critchley, *Infinitely Demanding*. See also p. 23 of this book.

It can go further. Through her we wonder about others, and other claims press on us. Should I begin to work for a wider social justice to help other claimants? Is he an ex-serviceman whom we did not collectively support when he returned damaged from a war to which we (maybe) assented? What should I do about that? And so on. In short, the claim can indeed feel virtually limitless, infinite. It is an experience which appears to carry universal ideals and responsibilities. That is why it is something Critchley can only describe as a "god-like" claim, even though he does not believe in God. It is the infinite quality of moral experience which has driven him to this quasi-religious language—as indeed it did for Plato and Kant before him.

To be clear, I do not mean we all routinely experience the moral impulse as this infinite claim pressing on us. I'm not suggesting this sort of moral intensity is normal experience. What many of us feel morally in routine day-to-day acts and decisions is probably little different from the sort of feeling we have about what we had for lunch. We may be generally nourished by an underlying sense of right and wrong, but hardly overwhelmed by the taste of it all the time. We are not normally sensing moral choice as this unique, intense, authoritative, infinite demand compelling us to metaphysical reflection. Put another way, we are not all Hamlets, Lears, Othellos, Antigones, constantly torn with tragic moral angst. I suspect we are mostly operating more like Shakespeare's wise fools, dealing with reality more pragmatically, just trying to move things on to the next scene. And that is just as well. No one can live all the time with too much intensity! However what we *routinely* experience morally is not the chief point here. My main concern is the underlying texture of morality. That, like the taste of lunch, is not always apparent on the surface of life, but it certainly does surface in extreme situations of good or evil. And that is where its infinite demand is apparent. That, along with its distinctiveness, authority and energy, is what presses the question. Just what *is* this? What is its ultimate origin?

Moral Meaning and God

So where now does this survey take us? Can it take us from these descriptions of moral sense to further explanation? What for instance about the repeated question about its ultimate origin? Is there any answer?

There is of course no consensus, not even for the question, let alone its answer. Yet there *is* a historic answer. That is, there is a view that has presented itself consistently and persuasively over many centuries, and across many cultures. It has done so not least because it is, at one level, so straightforward. It is the simple answer of theism. It is the view that what we are encountering in this unfulfillable moral ideal with its unique authority is what even Critchley found himself half-driven to, in spite of himself. Namely, when we meet the moral sense we are actually meeting the mind and will of a personal God.

This intimate connection between moral sense and theistic sense is, in my view, the most enduring and convincing of all traditional bridges between general human experience and God. And it is particularly clear in the particular phenomenology of actual moral experience just offered. What, after all, is this unique energy of the push and pull of this moral impulse most *like*? It is precisely like meeting another mind and will. To meet a powerful and attractive personality is to feel their mind, will, desires, impinging on us in just the way a strong moral claim does. Their own mind and will intrinsically exercises a kind of claim on ours. We are repelled from what we sense they do not want, and attracted towards what we sense they do want. So when we then experience this same push and pull in a uniquely energetic, authoritative and "infinite" form, it is natural to see it not just as the will of another human individual, nor even just of society, but as the will of a personal God.

To be sure, because the notion of a personal divine will is now widely rejected on other grounds this will not always convince. Far from it. And even for the religiously minded there may be reticence or embarrassment about naming moral experience in this way, as an encounter with God. We may even be embarrassed to own up to such a strong sense of moral claim just in its own terms, let alone as a religious experience. This is not surprising, bearing in mind the abusive role that moral certainties can play, with or without religious sanction. Even so it remains notable how persuasively the one suggests the other even when we are reluctant to accept it. Ernest Hemingway's fictional character Robert Jordan speaks for many in this respect. He says his moral feeling of "consecration to a duty toward all of the oppressed of the world" was "as difficult and embarrassing to speak about as a religious experience."[4] Yet the fact remains both that he *had* that sense, and that he felt its religious force.

A divine origin for moral sense does not for one moment mean that only the religiously inclined experience the moral claim fully or respond to it. That is palpably not the case. Nor would it mean that any of us experience its content reliably. Of course not. This moral impulse, whatever its ultimate origin, is always shaped for better or worse by our surrounding culture and distorted by our flawed humanity. That is why there is moral disagreement, and abuses of moral certainty. But this *form* of the moral impulse, however flawed its content, nonetheless remains God-like, for all the reasons suggested. It is the cumulative effect of all these features of the moral sense in our experience just described. They certainly offer this clear connection, even if they cannot prove it.

Moral Sense and Practical Living

This connection can moreover have practical not just theoretical implications. They are implications which arise from the general disposition that this metaphysical worldview can form in us, both personally and socially. It offers an orientation to life which is genuinely distinctive, with more resources than some others for the hard challenges of the moral life.

---

4. Hemingway, *For Whom the Bell Tolls*.

So for example, a thinner worldview of a purely reduction-ist or solely socio-biological account of morality faces inevitable limits when faced with the moral demand. By definition, because it has no further grounding and meaning, it has fewer resources to offer us. This is most likely to have an effect when we are struggling with our natural weakness of the will, our predisposition to miti-gate the moral demand. In these circumstances a demand which has no distinctive meaning or ultimate grounding is bound to lose some authority. In contrast, this "thicker" worldview with its sense of metaphysical ultimacy can offer more resources. It is not that metaphysical or religious commitments necessarily provide more effective moral rules or principles for coping with them. Nor, as I have insisted, do they guarantee any better moral perception or fuller response in any particular individual. But its orienta-tion towards the ultimate and perfect should still help *generally* shape the expectation of what moral effort can be made. It should at least predispose us to look for more ways of meeting a moral demand. It should also make us less satisfied with the immediate constraints or weaknesses we may have. A metaphysical or divine weight behind a moral claim cannot but help in pressing us to per-sist beyond normal limits. And where it cannot achieve that it, its energy may at least push us to attain different kinds of moral goals (discussed more later).

This thicker worldview can also help us deal more construc-tively with moral failure and compromise.[5] This may seem coun-ter-intuitive. *Prima facie*, an absolute, perfectionist, and objective sense of moral idealism might be expected only to highlight the inevitability of failure and compromise. To name a moral impulse as an ultimate and infinite claim, it might seem, can only set us up to fail in absolute terms, crushing us with the weight of it. Com-promises fare no better. They may be noble attempts to mitigate failure but by definition they still fail an infinite and perfectionist demand. Weakness of the will and the intrinsic structure of the world (both its social and "natural" reality) will always limit our moral reach at some point so, however hard-won and laudable, a

5. See further White, "Idealism and Compromise."

compromise is still always "falling short."[6] This is potentially just as crushing.

Yet this is not at all the only possible outcome. In fact, a wider worldview can reframe failure quite differently.[7] Belief in the ultimacy and objectivity of moral sense can actually offer release from the weight of failure and the disappointments of compromise. Why? Because it releases us from ultimate responsibility. This follows naturally from the wider metaphysical view that we are not the only origin of this ultimate demand. If this impulse to perfection comes not just from our own minds or society but also from a transcendent moral demand ("God" for some) we cannot be finally responsible for fulfilling it. As finite creatures, not ourselves the ultimate creators, there are limits both to our reach and to our responsibility. This does not detract from the authority of the claim and its pull on us to respond strenuously. But it reframes Kant's dictum at a crucial point. An absolute "ought" does *not* imply an ultimate "can." And that in turn means it cannot imply responsibility for perfection.

To be sure, we may operate with this sort of disposition anyway to some extent, regardless of metaphysical or religious commitments. Most of us know all too well that we live with some limits over which we have no control. Just by living longer and growing older we have come to know we are constrained by dependencies and limits imposed on us by our genes, our upbringing, our culture. Given a naturally pragmatic temperament we may then instinctively reach for this as a liberating insight and (Eliot-like) be content just to do our best. The point remains, however, that a metaphysical or theistic foundation for morality adds a further dimension to such realism. To know ourselves as creatures not only of our genes, our parents, and our culture, but also of an ultimate reality ("God"), frames our dependency even more radically. Correlatively, the release from the angst of thinking *we* can ever achieve it all will also be more radical. We are freed once for

6. Cf. Rom 3:23.

7. For example see Jaspers, *Tragedy Is Not Enough*, which hints at a non-theistic metaphysical framework for this.

all from the humanist burden of belief in inevitable progress, the myth of rationalism and scientific socialism that we alone can ever eventually meet all our ideals individually or collectively.

With this overall worldview we should then be able to operate instinctively with a character and disposition which strives to the utmost, but which is also less arrogant and more realistic. That is the genius of this worldview. It combines both. It is precisely because the claim of this wider worldview comes from beyond the limits of our own social constructions or biological reality that it can *both* maintain its claim on us even when its claims are not met, *and* release us from ultimate responsibility and the burden of needing to succeed. This is undoubtedly a resource. It helps maintain moral energy even when our goals have failed. It can steer us to redirect energy constructively, rather than despair when it is thwarted.

The importance of this is particularly apparent if we are tempted to a kind of tragic self-referential response to our limits and failures. This self-referential response is a familiar trap. When failing to meet our ideals it is all too easy to find satisfaction instead in the sense of *heroic* failure, painting ourselves proudly as victims of forces beyond our control which at least we had tried to overcome. But it is a flawed reaction to compromise or failure precisely because it deflects our efforts into our own self-justification, rather than continuing to pursue the original endeavor more realistically, or in some other way.

Political rhetoric from recent history (where we have some critical distance) offers numerous examples of this. From the left, for example, consider the rhetoric of the UK miners at the time of the strikes in the 1980s, and from the right (before Brexit) some of the rhetoric about Europe. In both cases protagonists aimed at a sincerely perceived good. In the first case, the aim was to secure benefits for miners in relation to impending pit closures. In the second, then aim was to secure (perceived) benefits for the British people in relation to European hegemony. In both cases, when each of these conflicted with other goals of the time and their aim was unrealized (that is, survival of the pits, or major concessions from Europe), there was failure. That is not surprising, possibly inevitable. But the issue is not so much the failure itself, rather how that failure was represented by the protagonists. It was largely portrayed as heroic tragedy. Leaders represented themselves going down fighting righteously. Thereby they displaced any effort to achieve at least some dimension of the original goal in other more realistic ways. Another example can be taken from the political center, in the context of the West's invasion of Iraq. All the same dynamics were there in the UK government's reaction to the long-term failure of the invasion. A leader cast himself in a heroic mold, insisting on good intentions and his own integrity even when the outcome was disastrous. But that very sense of rightness then tended to deflect further constructive efforts to pursue the cause in any other way.

By contrast, a recognition that the ultimate origin and responsibility for all true ideals lies beyond us, whether in objective moral law or in the mind of God, renders these self-regarding responses ridiculous. It frees us as nothing else can from the fantasy that we always have to be seen to succeed. In place of that fantasy, the more realistic, relaxed, humble character which this metaphysic should form in us is then free to have its effect. To emphasize again, this effect is not to diminish our motivation. On the contrary, it increases it because the sense of a distinctive, authoritative, irreducible claim on us remains unyielding. As Critchley notes, it is not easy to dilute or deflect. The difference is that it calls us to persist, whatever measure of success we do or do not have, simply by its own power of attraction rather than by our own self-regard. In this way it also necessarily leads us to seek other ways, and other helpers, for our moral endeavors. So it is creative, as well as humbling and unyielding.

There is an even more energizing effect in any specifically Christian worldview which includes the hope of redemption. To see pressing ideals not just as an abstract moral demand but as the will of a personal God carries this further promise that our inevitable compromises and failures can be positively redeemed, not just cast aside or bypassed. An abstract cause or ideal, however nobly and powerfully it motivates us, cannot support us nor can it forgive when we fail. It can only ignore (or condemn). But a personal and redeeming God can both support and forgive. S/he can pick us up and keep us pressing forward rather than withdrawing, giving up, or just fantasizing heroically. So it is a belief which offers unique resources to persist even after repeated failure. This is the even greater genius of a specifically religious worldview. In the face of thwarted ideals and sense of moral failure it can repeatedly combine both a sense of release, continued motivation, and support, all within a coherent narrative.

A Positive Example?

How realistic is all this? Are these dispositions, and practical outcomes, ever to be found in real lives? Are there any narratives which embody them? There are, though not always easy to find. Often they can be identified in unsung lives lived humbly, known only to a few, but evident to any with eyes to see. We are all likely to know someone of this kind. In public life it may be harder to find. "Doing God" in public life, or just owning explicit metaphysical moral commitments, is not always admitted. Even so it exists.

A notable exemplar, for instance, was Dag Hammarskjold, second Secretary General of the United Nations.[8] He never paraded his faith, but it is clear from his diary and letters that he was deeply formed in character and dispositions by a rich inner life of religious reflection on the ideals he held. What is particularly clear is how he experienced this moral demand in the divine will. It was not, for him, a series of edicts and principles which could all be perfectly kept, but precisely the experience of a personal encounter which would continually inspire him through a long narrative of trying, failing, and trying again. So in responding to the moral demand in this complex world Hammarskjöld was not just trying to follow principles or undertake an examination in ethical logic, attempting the impossible task of reconciling conflicting principles. He was experiencing the moral impulse precisely as response to a person, a divine personal reality who was inspiring, shaping, and

8. Cf. Lipsey, *Hammarskjöld.*

forming his character over time, continually forgiving and restoring him in his attempts.

It is also clear that Hammarskjöld never saw himself as anything more than just one partner in this moral enterprise. While taking as much responsibility as he could and should, he never assumed total responsibility. He was sharing in projects which he knew he alone would never solve. Part of the release and motivation he experienced within this religious frame of reference was precisely rooted in this trust that God took ultimate responsibility, able to continue the moral work and its motivation through others where he fell short. This is the full measure of what motivated him both to enter the minefields of Gaza, Suez, the Congo Crisis, and Cold War tensions, and to persist purposively even when exhausted, vilified, and apparently defeated by intractable circumstances. It was not just abstract principles of justice, democracy, and freedom but this sense of summons and support provided by a personal relationship with a divine source of *all* moral meaning and all moral effort. This kept motivating him, sustaining his efforts and allowing him to persist without becoming cynical, fantasizing, or retreating to self-aggrandizement. It is captured in numerous fragments we have from his letters and diary: in spite of impossibilities all that matters is "the slow building up of what we are [all] striving for" and our capacity to "vanish as an end, and remain purely as a means."[9] It is the exact opposite from heroic posturing.

Here we see the moral impulse allowed its full metaphysical meaning with its unique character and authority having real effect in praxis. The character and disposition it sustained was both realistic about our limits, yet also always pressing forward in the moral endeavor. It was a disposition which always saw the point and possibility in moral effort, even when "the eye sees further than the hand can reach."[10] Again I stress, none of this is meant to imply that only those with explicit metaphysical commitments

9. Lipsey, *Hammarskjöld*, 543.

10. A maxim used by Karl Deutsch in his appreciation of the philosophy of Karl Jaspers.

have this disposition, nor that those who do espouse them always benefit from them. That is demonstrably not the case. But it does help unfold the potential range of its meaning, wherever and in whomever we encounter it.

Creative Fidelity—An Excursus

Such, then, are some general features of moral sense, its potential source, and the overall disposition this might shape in us. They all convey something of what we mean by "moral." They outline something of its overall texture and offer at least something of a possible explanation for it, drawing primarily from the way it presents in our experience.

But can the moral sense also be exemplified in even more specific ways? Could we see it concretely embodied in more specific issues of ordinary life? A single life such as Hammerskjold can ground it to some extent. But that is only one life. It is anecdotal. Can we do more than that, and delineate a more systematic grounding for it in a specific moral disposition which would illuminate more situations?

To pursue this requires more than this essay. It belongs to another remit altogether. Yet as an excursus perhaps one exemplar could be noted. So I venture the notion of "faithfulnes." It is a vital disposition. Although not fashionable, it lies at the heart of any flourishing personal or social moral order. And in this context it will work well as an example of how this moral demand unfolds in concrete ways. It demonstrates how these general features of the moral sense can actually work in ordinary life, and particularly in our current social context.[11]

---

11. Cf. White, *Identity* where the notion of fidelity is explored, and at greater length. Twenty years on I find it more, not less, apposite.

The Context of Rapid and Radical Change

This context, first, is significant and needs outlining. It is the intensity and peculiar nature of *change* we experience in late-modern social life. Rapid and interconnected change caused by new information technology, social media, cultural globalization, the economic drive to stimulate constant new consumer demand, is pervasive. It is also powerful in its effects, and has dramatic potential. It is potentially a creative force for good. It also has potential for damage, division, and de-stabilization. Its potential, either way, is radical because the effects are not trivial or merely functional for human living. It is ontological. It affects our being and identity, our sense of who we are. And so it is a context in which effective moral dispositions are clearly going to be vital.

The issues it presents need elaborating. One reason this kind of change is so formative, for example, is because it starts early. Children and young people are not now just passively receiving the impact of changing ideas and images (e.g., through terrestrial TV). In addition they interact actively online with an even wider world of change. They can intimately connect at any time of day or night with a multitude of other changing anonymous virtual bloggers and game players, from anywhere in the world. It is an experience from which they can absorb lifestyles, political views, values, prejudices which relativize everything previously inherited, and which offers instead a multitude of new identities.

This condition of "*liquid* modernity," as sociologist Zygmunt Bauman described it, typifies adult life too.[12] We are all exposed through various media to a torrent of options. It is so formative because it is not just about different goods to buy, but about deeper lifestyle priorities, beliefs, values. These unsettle our settled family structures, our allegiance to institutions, religions, moralities, local communities, and so they affect our sense of who we are. This may not only disturb and change us directly but also indirectly through the change it brings in others around us in family, friends, colleagues. This too may destabilize us. So when for example I find

12. Bauman, *Liquid Modernity*.

48

I can no longer relate to my neighbour as husband of his first wife, teacher, Labour supporter—but now as partner of his new male friend, software consultant, politically detached—who I am in relation to him also changes. Multiply this with others, and I am affected even more.

We should not underestimate how disturbing this can be. Not knowing who we are or who other people are in a settled way, always being on the cusp of the unknown with others and ourselves, can evoke a sense of loss, fear, disintegration, mortality. It is a cause of high rates of stress in individuals. It is also a cause of strain in society generally. Family, civic life, and institutional life, which depend on relatively settled values, continuities and commitments, tend to crumble without them. That is why "change and *decay*," as a famous Christian hymn puts it, often seem to go together.

This is not for one moment to suggest all change is destructive, and decay is all we see. Emphatically not. Change and re-invention of ourselves is also, of course, a vital source of creativity, liberation, life. A fixed, frozen, *un*changing persona in individuals is often a sign of spiritual death, whereas change in ourselves is often a sign of spiritual life. Socially, too, change is often progressive. It can free us from false identities imposed on us by oppressive social systems. Social change has freed women from fixed roles determined by men, and freed gay people from discrimination. Changes in education, refusing to pigeon-hole children with fixed identities of intellectual and social potential at an early age, allow them to flourish with later development and lifelong learning. This sort of fluidity and change is clearly positive. Seeing all change as threat also fails the simple test of history. Rapid change happened in the past and we did not disintegrate then. As critic Frank Kermode has pointed out, much of our current fluid social condition is just a mirror of social revolutions of the nineteenth century, many of which brought benefits.[13]

Even so, we also need to acknowledge a distinctive and potentially dangerous twist to the particular nature of change we now experience. This lies in the fact that much current change is without any clear direction; we do not have any sense of where

13. Kermode, "Waiting for the End."

we are heading with it. This is a function of the wider social and cultural location we inhabit, commonly called postmodernity, in which we have largely lost confidence in any agreed overall stories to help us deal with or interpret change. Although overall stories of life offered by science, politics, cultural theory and religion remain available, none now commands any real consensus. They are fragmented by pluralism. This means that when a new idea or experience occurs there is no agreed coherent story by which we can evaluate its meaning. Instead we are left to create a meaning for ourselves, and purely self-chosen meanings are bound to be more fragile, transient, isolating.

This presents challenges. Leaving things just to our own preference in this way makes us vulnerable to stress. It also makes us vulnerable to a counter-reaction, and to manipulation by others. The stress of plurality drives some to the certainties of authoritarianism, totalitarianism and tribalism. It is an attempt to replace the confusions of choice with a place where shared values and lifestyles are reinforced rather than relativized, and where difference is then demonized. The genuine attraction of this sort of certainty to a strained and fragmented self is evident. It is also cynically exploited by religious and political ideologues needing to enlist support, or by those just pursuing their own corporate or personal financial gain. In other words, leaving us free with only our personal preferences does not necessarily make us free at all. We are likely to become prey either just to our own fickle feelings, or to others who manipulate us.

Creative Fidelity as a Response to Change

So in this context of change and instability what then constitutes a truly *moral* response? It is precisely here that a creative fidelity (which I shall define shortly) presents itself. Although currently unfashionable, it actually has longstanding moral pedigree.[14]

14. It has Judaeo-Christian roots, amongst others. Cf. Alasdair MacIntyre's seminal analysis of social instability in *After Virtue* where he makes a cryptic call for a new "Benedict" to save us. Benedict developed a rule of life for a

Above all, it bears all the hallmarks of moral meaning discussed above. Properly understood, it can claim irreducible and persistent authority across a range of circumstances. It can offer an ideal pattern of living which continues to summon us "infinitely" but also realistically, regardless of profound practical difficulties. It is particularly apposite in our current context because it offers stability for our identity through the experience of change, yet without denying change. And it is sufficiently grounded in a collective worldview to give it more staying power than purely personal preference, yet also sufficiently flexible to survive in a plural world.

Creative fidelity has two key elements. First, it is a serious, sustained, and (if necessary) sacrificial commitment to the wellbeing of a person or institution holistically and through time. It is commitment through a long and "wide" narrative. In other words, it is commitment to the well-being of someone, some institution or enterprise, both in terms of their past, present, future, and in their relation to others—not just in relation to an individual's well-being here and now. This sort of fidelity is what uniquely gives identity and stability to unstable people and institutions through time and change. It also gives identity to the one being faithful. It is a commitment, as philosopher Josiah Royce said, which unifies a life, giving it "centre, fixity, stability."[15] Faithfulness in this sense becomes a virtuous circle replace the vicious circle of destabilization for all concerned. Without this sort of faithfulness we splinter into a thousand fragments.[16] With it we can all recover solidity, integrity, stability.

The vital second element, however, is that it also has fluidity. This commitment is not just a matter of doggedly "being there" for someone, some cause, or some institution, long-term. It means being *creatively* there for them. It means being willing to look for new ways to relate constructively to that wider narrative of the other's life. In other words, it is not a disposition which simply locks us

monastic community in his own unstable times which bears wider scrutiny for other times, perhaps even all times. "Creative fidelity" is one characterization of that rule. See MacIntyre, *After Virtue*.

15. Royce, *Philosophy of Loyalty*, 863.

16. See Kundera, *Unbearable Lightness of Being*, 87.

into an unchanging attitudes, absolute rules, unyielding dogmas. It is certainly not blind loyalty. It is much more dynamic and critical, if necessary, in its constancy. French Catholic philosopher Gabriel Marcel, who coined the phrase "creative fidelity," describes it as a creative changing response to the presence of another person (or institution) who themselves are alive and changing.[17] So it harnesses change, even requires change, to deal with change. It is a disposition which incorporates the positive role of change even in its attempt to re-establish stability. That is why it can maintain its claim to moral authority even in changing and challenging circumstances. As an overall disposition it can remain binding and authoritative precisely because of its fluidity and creativity.

As for examples of where we may now see all this at work? Two key areas of personal and public life suggest themselves. They are both arenas for serious moral endeavor where change is rife, and our sense of identity profoundly implicated. Both are areas of potential strain as well as profound satisfaction. And both cry out for this disposition of creative fidelity. First, the ordering of our close personal relationships of friendship, sexual partnership, marriage, family life. Second, more briefly, the ordering of our working relationships and practices.

Creative Fidelity in Close Personal Relationships

Social patterns of personal relationship and kinship have, of course, always changed. Kinship patterns in particular have always been shifting. But not always at the present rate and in this apparently directionless way which we now experience. Sociologist Anthony Giddens did particularly useful work on this in the 1990s which still resonates.[18] The fundamental change he suggested in all our personal relationships, even family relationships, is a shift

17. Marcel, *Being and Having*; Marcel, *Creative Fidelity*.

18. Giddens, *Consequences of Modernity*; Giddens, *Modernity and Self-Identity*. Subsequent studies are legion, sometimes critical but often acknowledging a debt to Giddens. Cf. Held and Thompson, *Social Theory of Modern Societies*.

towards a more "reflexive," self-referential project. This means we now tend to choose, assess, and fashion our relationships more in terms of their direct impact on our own personal experience than as part of a wider public or social role or duty. One outcome is that we are more likely to end relationships when they do not quickly deliver that personal experience we want.

Like all social trends, this is likely to be ephemeral, at least in some respects. Giddens's analysis already needs qualification. For instance, while social media has intensified some aspects of self-referential trends, emerging generations are also now being formed by a renewed sense of interdependence (not least with the natural environment). Identity is now pursued and constructed more collectively, as well as individually. Even so, the overall trajectory described as reflexivity has hardly disappeared. Although it may now be tempered by other social commitments it persists, and a measure of this lies in the public consequences of these trends. There is an increase in single-parent families, absent fathers, non-marital births, a profusion of different forms of temporary cohabitation, and decrease in some long-term relationships. It has also had consequences for the private texture of our experience of relationships. This is harder to identify, but Giddens tried and again his suggestions still resonate. His observation is that this change has generated relationships of more intensity, excitement, and more emotional honesty. At the same time, they also tend to be more unstable, inward-looking, less engaged with their status as public roles.

Evaluating these changes is not straightforward. There are potential gains. A desire for inward intensity has unlocked new honesty and satisfaction compared to the formalized emotionally frozen nature of some past forms of fixed relationship. As noted, fluidity in identity and personal relationships has given new possibilities for gay and transgender people, and it has meant liberation for women previously locked into oppressive relationships. Yet as Giddens and others have indicated we have also seen the destabilizing effects of these changes in personal stress and social damage. The quest for short-term self-referring emotional intensity and satisfaction may mean we cut and run quickly to find a new relationship when that satisfaction fades, rather than staying to discover new satisfactions *within* an existing one. This entails those obvious consequences of many transient relationships. Children in particular may be damaged by the insecurity this brings. Elderly dependants too may be neglected because unable to provide that sort of reciprocal intensity of relationship. Anyone, of any age or gender, can be damaged simply because of the pressure of a high emotional expectation and the threat of transience in any relationship. Swiftly forming new relationships and roles to meet these expectations may then simply cause more stress, breakdown, feeding yet more instability into our relationships. It is a potentially vicious circle.

To be sure this is not a picture, either for better or worse, of all actual relationships. But it is a real and observable trend, and creates a context in which the disposition of creative fidelity has extraordinary relevance. A disposition whose instinctive goal is not just short-term transient satisfaction for ourselves, but the much more interesting and satisfying project of sharing the long-term narrative of someone else's life creatively, provides an alternative which is realistic and constructive. It is credible and realistic because while an overall orientation to long-term commitment may be (temporarily) counter-cultural, it is not simply proposing relationships with fixed rules; it is providing a creative and dynamic response, fitting well with a fluid culture as well as challenging it. It is constructive in its potential for healing the damage caused by instability, while still endorsing the positive gains of change and fluidity.

A key test, of course, will be the hard cases for commitment. Can fidelity retain its moral authority, obligation, and energy, when circumstances are at their most challenging? Can any sense be made of creative faithfulness in situations of irretrievable marital breakdown? Can creative fidelity be maintained with someone in the last stages of dementia when personality has wholly changed? These are harrowing (and always particular) circumstances, sadly not rare, and they can certainly strain commitment to breaking point.

Yet the claim that fidelity can still have meaning remains credible if we remember the full range of this disposition. In particular we need to recall how it holds us to seeing the *whole* narrative of someone's life, not just the current state or most recent episode. In the case of severe dementia creative fidelity may help maintain *some* form of relationship precisely by helping us see the person not only as they are with us now but as they once were (and, with Christian faith, how they will be in eternity). In the case of losing a partner by irretrievable breakdown, the wider narrative can again help in maintaining some form of relatedness. It can be transformative to be able to see a former partner not just as they are in their present relations with us but also as they have been, and might be in the future, in their relations with us *and others.* They are not only the person who has changed or left us now but also the person who is the continuing father or mother of the children, the continuing friend of our friends. This wider narrative offers an opportunity to honor the relationship constructively in some way, even when its previous form has ended. It offers a way of maintaining a kind of creative fidelity in the hardest of circumstances.

This is not fantasy. In the context of dementia, non-cognitive and non-verbal bonds to evoke deep memory (touch, music, smell etc) are increasingly shown to maintain at least some kind of relationship. In the case of family breakdown, new and constructive social patterns to facilitate this creative fidelity have also emerged, and demonstrably so.[19] Former couples have created different forms of loyalty to previous partners by formalizing patterns of communication between stepfamilies in new social conventions of expected social interaction, a way of continuing to honor previous relationships and thereby creating new forms of social stability. Currently this may be sporadic. But if this disposition of creative fidelity becomes more embedded as a social norm, not just as individual choice, these practices become more thinkable and more widespread. Social morality and religious morality could combine to good effect here. Traditional ideals of lifelong commitment in

19. Some foundational research was carried out in the late twentieth century. See Stacey, *Brave New Families.*

marriage need not be abandoned altogether if supplemented by a willingness to recognize new forms of creative fidelity when that commitment fails. To embody this positively in new cultural and social forms (including, for the religious, a new liturgy for both divorce and remarriage) will cement overall stability rather than undermine it. Being able to embrace a new partnership *and* some form of continuing fidelity to previous partners can help prevent the vicious circle of yet another splintered family within stepfamilies.

In short, in this difficult and fluid arena of human relationships and kinships here is a disposition which works, and which maintains credibility in the hardest of circumstances. "Creative Fidelity" is demonstrating just that binding authority and personal energy which marks the distinctively moral.

Creative Fidelity in Working Practices

The other arena to consider, more briefly, is our working relationships and practices. It is a similar area of human experience in many respects, not least as a place where our identity may be both profoundly formed and called into question. It is also site of change which can be a catalyst both of profound stress and deep satisfaction. And it is an arena in which creative fidelity is again apt and potentially transformative.

Here too change is hardly new, nor the potential stress it causes. But recent developments in management theory, rapid developments in information technology, and economic drivers, have all contributed to an increasing rate of it. One of the key overall changes is from settled occupations (whether land-based, industrial-based, tech-based, or commercial) to portfolio work, short-term consultancy, project-based work. There has also been an associated shift from collective place-based work to more flexible and potentially isolated home-based work, accelerated by the 2020 pandemic.

Cumulatively these changes have had consequences which mirror in many ways the changes in our close personal relationships, and prompt a similarly mixed evaluation. On the one hand it has freed up labor, bringing economic benefit to companies and personal benefits of intense short-term satisfaction when individual projects come to fruition. On the other hand this fluidity has also produced a hollowed out and more pressured work culture, bereft of long-term personal loyalties and trust, undermining the worth, satisfaction, and identity of belonging long-term to companies and institutions. Even when the rhetoric of loyalty and belonging to a team is employed this is often spurious (as business analysts readily concede), chiefly because the culture actually depends on short-term, shifting relationships.

The trend has been significant for some time. Surveys of managerial careers have long reported that project-based work and fluidity of employment leads to an environment that lacks the long-term relational contracts which require mutual commitment and trust over a long period.[20] They have highlighted the way in which the passion involved in achieving particular personal goals now largely replaces real loyalty to the people or institutions.[21] It is a culture in which personal strain is evident. This is not only the strain of insecurity but an even deeper rupture of our identity. Where a work culture requires me to operate with radically different values at work and home (e.g., working for short-term personal success in the former, long-term sharing of life in the latter) then sooner or later I disintegrate.

This is not of course a picture of all work experience. But it remains an observable trajectory. And as such it surely presents itself as another obvious arena for creative fidelity or loyalty (a more recognizable term in this context). A default disposition of loyalty in both employer and employee can help recover satisfactions of long-term mutual achievement. At the same time, if it is *creative* loyalty, it will not become a fossilizing disposition of inertia, stifling the economic and personal advantages of change. Instead it can be a bedrock *for* change. It will provide the sort of stable personal relationships at work which generate an identity

20. Heriot and Pemberton, *New Deals.*
21. E.g., Demos Report, *Entrepreneurship and the Wired Life.*

that binds the enterprise collectively but which also generate an energy, purpose, and confidence which can critique the operation. This contrasts with short-term purely target-driven contractual relationships which purport to motivate more but can actually dissipate energy, creativity, confidence through the stress of insecurity and fractured identity. It offers instead this constructive endorsement of change and innovation precisely by containing it within this structure of overall trust and stability.

Again, this is not fantasy. Companies and institutions can and do attempt to honor the narrative of their workers' and members' lives by offering longer term career progression, with training. This means that an individual's identity and gifts at work are not atomized, exploited just for the present then cast aside, but offered continuity and harnessed to other areas of work. Some employers also now honor the wider narrative of a worker's life by encouraging social engagement, volunteering, wider public duty, so that work values and personal values of the employee are more integrated. These are already genuine "new deals" at work which offer practical structures for creative loyalty, and the language of building trust with employees and clients is commonly seen as pragmatic business sense.[22] So here again we see in fidelity a moral disposition which can work, and which can be binding, in a range of situations. Its moral credentials are sound.

The Moral Core of Creative Fidelity—Realism and Roots

To be sure, this appeal to a binding disposition of fidelity will be contested, like any moral principle. But one reason why I believe it can be sustained—at work or in any other field—is because it connects with human psychology at a most basic level. It is wanted as well as needed. In other words, "commitment" is actually nothing like as universally unfashionable or counter-cultural as it may

22. Literature on the nature and purpose of corporate relationships is now legion. *The Harvard Business Review* on customer loyalty (2011) is now complemented by much wider concerns for building relationships, e.g., Burgess, *Executive Engagement Strategies*.

seem. In spite of the pressures of late-modern consumer society and the short-term purely self-satisfying instincts of human nature (evolutionary or just plain sinful), we do retain longings for commitments in life.[23] We want to give some expression to our underlying connectedness with others and dependence on them, as with the environment.

This suggests why fidelity will indeed work as a realistic as well as truly moral demand. It is precisely as a disposition which can connect with our will and desires as well as challenging them, that it has moral credibility. By presenting itself as binding and authoritative but also engaged with who we really are, it has credible authority. And by showing itself as adaptable within the overall binding commitments it wants to express, it bears a further mark of (moral) realism. In these ways it is offering exactly what credible moral meaning seems to require; an apparently objective, authoritative, claim on us which transcends the particular desires or needs either of any one individual or society, yet also able to relate effectively and universally to them.

It also has the authority of moral history. That is, it has deep roots not just in human psychology but in social history. In fact creative fidelity has a very clear traceable historical lineage in the Western tradition. The crucible for it lies in pre-Socratic Greek philosophy, in the debate between Heraclitus and Parmenides and the sort of world which, between them, they perceived. Heraclitus saw flux, difference, change as the very stuff of all reality, the very womb of all life; Parmenides, and later Plato, saw oneness, stability, consistency, as the necessary and ultimate ground of all this change. Within that symbiotic tension between flux and constancy creative fidelity has an obvious if implicit source, as a rare moral disposition which actually works universally in this sort of complex world. It then received further explicit grounding, and huge impetus, in the development of Christian faith when theologians saw the same tension between flux and constancy in God. By insisting on God as Trinity, as an eternal interplay of three interrelated persons in oneness, they combined both flux and stability

23. Cf. Farley, *Personal Commitments.*

as ultimates in God's own being. Dynamic faithfulness is then the correlate in the divine character.

This is concretely expressed in the narratives of Scripture where God constantly projects his/her identity in the history of Israel, and in the person of Christ, precisely as a God of creative fidelity who combines flux and stability. These narratives consistently show who God is ("I am who I am"/ "I will be who I will be") in the way God keeps long-term covenant faith with people. They demonstrate a love shown through time, which is the essence of faithfulness. God is one who kept faith with them even in wilderness and exile with a consistent character, unlike the other capricious gods around. God is then shown in Christ as one who kept faith even at the cost of the cross, undeterred by betrayal, desertion, death. It is a specifically *creative* fidelity throughout because in this long narrative God shows fidelity by doing new things, not simply by demonstrating an unchanging eternal essence (and the notion of God changing and doing new things is not metaphysically worrying precisely because a Trinitarian God can uniquely combine flux with stability). In short, the seeds of this disposition lie both in ancient Greek and Hebrew worldviews and in a creative Christian synthesis of these. And for Western moral and social tradition this is exactly where moral authority has most of its roots.

To be sure, this sort of authority has now largely faded for many. But has the notion of faithfulness itself? It is true that recent intellectual history shows little interest, with only the early twentieth-century idealist philosopher Josiah Royce writing systematically much about it.[24] Even Christian theology seems to have had diminishing interest.[25] Fidelity generally seems to have become another casualty of post-liberal suspicions about fixity and the metanarratives of inertia. And yet, properly understood, there should be no inevitability about this. After all, this call to

24. Royce, *Philosophy of Loyalty*.

25. One notable exception in systematics in the mid-twentieth century was H. Richard Niebuhr. See Niebuhr, *Radical Monotheism and Western Culture*; cf. also Niebuhr, *Responsible Self*. Biblical theology has perhaps fared better. See, for example, Wright, *Paul and the Faithfulness of God*.

faithfulness is precisely *not* a reactionary call to fixity. It is not a failure of nerve in breaking out of the *status quo*, not just blind loyalty. What I hope to have made clear is the opposite. Creative fidelity is in fact a progressive, life-giving, healing, dynamic disposition, not at all reactionary or oppressive. It is a defensible and truly moral disposition which fits well in today's fluid climate, in a way which is both challenging and constructive. And it is also so deep-rooted in both our natural instincts for commitment and our historic constructed traditions that it is unlikely to remain suppressed for ever—whatever current social fashions prevail.

Creative Fidelity and Moral Meaning

All this, I trust, demonstrates creative fidelity as a telling example of moral meaning when given specific shape. The fundamental features of moral demand are all there. It summons us with a distinctive and compelling kind of call, character and authority which cannot easily be dismissed or deconstructed. It describes a disposition which is both realistic yet always pressing forward to an ideal. It is a summons which make sense particularly (though not exclusively) within a religious metaphysic, and historically it sits securely (though not exclusively) within the Christian religious tradition. Equally it does not require allegiance to either faith or metaphysics to be experienced as a key moral imperative, nor to be widely essayed in practice.

As for the form of moral meaning more generally, I end where we began. Kant's sense of wonder remains. Trying to unravel some of its features and identifying it in concrete form (such as fidelity) may unfold some of its meaning. But it does not demystify it altogether. It does not reduce its distinctive, compelling quality. It is still best characterized, I suggest, as a near-universal experience which is one of the most profound and fertile constituents of the human condition. It has metaphysical resonance which, along with spiritual meaning, aesthetics, and creativity, helps define what makes living most worthwhile. And so it surely lies very close to the heart of all meaning, all mattering, all true *living*.

Meanings of God

Our little systems have their day; They have their day and
cease to be ... And thou, O Lord, art more than they

ALFRED TENNYSON, *IN MEMORIAM*

IF THERE IS AN ultimate ground to meaning and morality, is this God? Does God lie as the shadow behind all meaning, and morality? Or rather, is God is the light which casts the shadow of all meaning, and morality? That is what faith believes. God is the ultimate source of both. But what then do we mean by God? What sort of reality is God? Is God a person, spirit, substance, a form of agency—or what? This is not the familiar question of much Western religion about the character of God (as compassionate, just, love, and so on). It is about the nature and meaning of God's being. It is a metaphysical question.

Perhaps we shouldn't even try to ask this sort of question. For at least two good reasons. The first simply because it's impossible. Rabbinic traditions like to tell the story of the visit of an emperor to a distinguished rabbi. "I should like to see thy God," said the emperor. "Impossible," said the rabbi. "But I will see Him!" insisted the emperor. So the rabbi led him out into the bright sunshine and pointed upwards. The emperor tried to look into the sun but could not. Its brightness blinded him and he bowed his head. The point is obvious. If God is absolute, transcendent, infinite, ultimate source of all reality, God will be in a different category to any reality we know in the world, which is relative, finite, transient. So God will not be knowable in any ordinary sense of the word. God, by definition, will be as impossible to grasp fully with human thought as the sun is impossible to see directly with human eyes.

This means all our attempts to imagine or talk about God will be bound to fail. In the face of infinity they will have to reduce God, scale God down to our size; they will anthropomorphize God. Or they will have to strain language to the point of meaninglessness: "the Father incomprehensible, the Son incomprehensible, the Holy Spirit incomprehensible" as the Christian Athanasian creed has it, where the intention may be to pay God some sort of metaphysical compliment but the effect is merely to address God as meaningless abstraction. Or else our words and thoughts will retreat to vacuous generalities; we dissolve God into just a spiritual ether of the universe, everywhere in general, nowhere and nothing in particular, characteristic of a good deal of contemporary spirituality in which experience of divinity lacks any specific form or content. In short, try to look into the meaning of God too closely and we end up either being too naïve, too abstract, or too vague.

So—better not to try at all? I understand that. Silence has its place, and there is a long and honorable tradition of reticence in the face of the mystery of God. Nonetheless I shall still try. I shall try simply because experiences and revelations believed to be of God, by their very nature, compel us to try. They are not neutral experiences. They do not leave us indifferent. Like pain, beauty, or the moral imperative, religious experiences and religious perceptions provoke some sort of reaction. They provoke at the very least an exclamation, even when explanation proves impossible. They also provoke action, sometimes contentiously. How then can we refuse to consider them more carefully? How can we not at least try to investigate the meaning of what lies behind them?

The second reason we might not try to describe God is that it begs a rather important prior question of whether God exists at all. This is hardly settled. It is more contested than ever in the twenty-first century. For many it is barely even worth contesting, so improbable does God seem. So should we not concentrate first on *this* debate? We could, and sometimes should. But again, this is not going to deter me from concentrating here instead on what we *mean* by God. After all, the reason why some believe in God and some do not so often depends precisely on what kind of God is under discussion. Preoccupying and unresolved debates about whether or not God exists which sidestep this have failed to grasp that questions of meaning may well need to precede questions of existence. Put simply, it really does help if we know what sort of reality it is whose existence we are disputing!

Persisting with the question of meaning therefore seems both right and necessary even for skeptics. And it is surely important for believers too. Is it not a matter of integrity for believers to consider more what *kind* of reality is being meant when we say we believe in God? The question is particularly urgent when images of God received through liturgy and childhood teaching have only bequeathed residual concepts of a very anthropomorphic reality who is simply incredible. Where "God" has been imaged as a person hovering over our world like a puppet master, intervening within it often by strange supernatural means, just what are we thinking? Do we really think of God like that? Perhaps not, when pressed. But then if we reject this crude mix of anthropomorphism and magic what *is* God like? How do we imagine or think of God credibly? The issue is often displaced by pragmatism. Within communities of faith talk of God is often only about the character of God and what we then believe God wants us (or the church) to do or be. But should we not sometimes face the question of what God him/herself *is*? Even if this is like looking into the sun, should we not at least try? For the sake of integrity I believe we should.

How then to proceed? It is tempting to cast the net widely. We could examine all world faiths, and look even more widely amongst popular spiritualities and religious philosophy. Keith Ward, former Regius Professor of Divinity at Oxford, for example, culls images for God from a wide-ranging quest through many religious traditions, poetry, and philosophy.[1] It is a fertile field to plough. Yet there is also some point in drilling down deeply instead into just one tradition, in this case, the Judaeo-Christian tradition. I will do this here. This is not because I am making a claim about its exclusivity. It is because I cannot do full justice to other faiths and do not wish to misrepresent them, whereas a focus on one tradition offers the opportunity of more rigor, at least within that field.

It is also because in fact there are huge and varied resources to probe even within this one faith. The one tradition is itself really a complex weave of many traditions with many faces of God, not just one. A multitude of meanings are generated within its Scriptures, even more within the poetry and philosophy inspired from it. God in Judaeo-Christian tradition is not only the Creator and Redeemer God of Israel's prophets and wilderness wanderings, and Father of Jesus Christ. God is also "the love that moves the sun," "the poet of the world," "the darkness between stars."[2] This is an expansive terrain, already more than enough to explore.

To help tackle this we shall need some frame to work with, so I shall use three of its most traditionally formative sources and take each in turn. I will trawl its Scriptures, its developed doctrine, and its literary and experiential mysticism. This is not the only way of doing it. A good case could be made for deeming its *practices* as a distinct source of meaning as well. But since Scripture, doctrine, and spiritual experience are already themselves interrelated outcomes of practice (as well as foundations for it) they will serve well enough.

Drama and Dialogue: Meanings of God in Scriptural Narrative

Scripture is an obvious place to begin. When meaning is sought, scriptural narratives are clearly foundational for this tradition. But they are not always straightforward. Since they rarely discuss

1. See for example Ward, *God.*
2. Ward, *God.*

meanings of God directly they have to convey meanings in other ways. They point to hidden meanings. and frequently convey meaning obliquely. This is crucial to grasp if we are trying to be faithful to the nature of Scripture generally, but especially its narratives which are more immediately about God. It is one of the most fatuous misunderstandings of the Bible that it characteristically presents us with very definite images for God, not least the crude anthropomorphic pictures of God bequeathed to us in some Bible teaching. In fact the Hebrew Bible in particular specifically *refuses* to offer definitive, precise, images of God. It insists on indirect ways of thinking and speaking of the divine. In its obliqueness it *is* still conveying meaning, but it is displaying God precisely as a reality beyond (normal) description or understanding. That is what "God" means.

This is not unlike the point being made by the rabbi to the emperor, but without the veto. Yes it is true that we cannot see the full sun directly, but we can still try to look because we can at least see some light in a refracted way. Take for example a seminal self-revelation of God to Moses in the Old Testament (Exod 33). Moses twice asks God to show himself and is refused. Instead, Moses is put in cleft of a rock, his face is covered with God's own hand, and all he is allowed as the glory of God passes by is a glimpse of the passing "backside" of God. It is a wonderfully suggestive picture. It is conveying how the full reality of the being of God is by its own intrinsic nature ("by his own hand") hidden from our complete grasp, but also how it is still a revelation which we may try to "see." There is a similar dialectic of seeing and not seeing in the New Testament where God's self-revelation is given in human form in the life and person of Christ. Jesus Christ is described as a unique embodiment of God, but also only as a "reflection" of God's glory, an "imprint" of God's being, an "image" of God (Heb 1:3; Col 1:15). Overall this affirms the unique significance of the encounter with Christ, but it also conveys a limit to our knowing in the encounter. The human figure of Jesus Christ, it seems, both *is* God within himself but also points to God beyond himself.

Metaphor, Metaphysics, Transcendence

In this awareness that ordinary thought and language fail to grasp God fully, Scripture is expressing a metaphysical truth, even though not written as metaphysics. It is conveying this view of the rabbi, that God is (*almost* blindingly) Other. God is a reality who transcends the ordinary more visible realities of this world. And this makes sense. As an infinite and ultimate ground of all things (i.e., as Creator) God cannot be of the same kind as any other thing. God cannot be a "thing" at all in the sense that anything in the world is. God cannot be a reality we can see, study, or represent, in the same way that we can describe any other object in the universe like the sea, sun, sodium chloride, symphony, or even a saint. Naturally we still have to use the language of ordinary things in the world to speak of God (it is the "hand" of God which hides)—what else is there to use? But this can only be a metaphorical or analogical use of language. "God" may be referred to in comparison to the things of this world but God is also always unlike them as well. The "hand" hides God as well as connects us to God.

This is important for the basic credibility of any God-talk, as well as its meaning. If we are truly trying to think of the meaning of God a sense of metaphysical mystery is patently more credible than any crassly literal description. Perhaps it is a familiar point. But it is still notable how metaphor and its implicit metaphysics belongs so essentially to Scripture itself, not just to the insights of later apparently more sophisticated theological reflection. And that is what is being emphasized here. This implicit metaphysics of transcendence is core to the meaning of God right within the earliest foundations of the tradition.

To be sure, it is not a consistent or unequivocal feature of Scripture. Scripture conveys God pre-eminently by dramatic narrative, not propositional philosophy, and in some narratives God seems neither so transcendent nor elusive. Anthropomorphism and premodern superstition are palpably present as well. The issue is sharpest in the world of the early Hebrew prophets. In 1 Samuel, for example, nomadic tribal prophets use mysterious objects to locate and discern the will of this God. "Urim" and "Thummim"—perhaps stones—seem to function in this way.[3] Elsewhere, especially in the older strands of the Hebrew Bible, prophets sing and dance to gain visions, and tell stories to interpret dreams, to claim God's will for the tribe has been directly revealed to them.

These narratives clearly portray an anthropomorphized and superstitious view of God. God appears here more like a force who can be "captured" in physical objects or human activity and manipulated to underwrite the identity and needs of the tribe. *Prima facie* there seems little difference here from the evidently fictional ancient gods of Homer in the *Iliad* or other tribal gods around them. As Homer's priests dug around in the entrails of goats to divine the will the gods for their tribal purposes of war, so Urim and Thummin were consulted to find out the will of Israel's God. In short, while some parts of biblical drama employ reticence, metaphor, mystery to acknowledge divine transcendence, others present a very different picture.

Even so, there is no equivalence. There is good warrant for prioritizing the more reserved images or transcendence over the cruder and superstitious images, not least because Scripture itself offers its own trajectories to support this. Within the biblical narratives there are pivotal moments of encounter with God which naturally establish a theological priority because they are distinctive moments in the development of faith. They are moments which demonstrate most clearly the qualitative difference from much surrounding religion, including some Hebrew religion. And, critically, these are precisely the main sites where we find that mystery, reserve, and a sense of transcendence. They are moments when, as Jewish literary critic Eric Auerbach points out, God is characteristically conveyed without physical location or description, unconfined, quite different to the over-defined and localized descriptions of the very human gods in (for example) Homeric literature.[4]

The pivotal role of these moments therefore establishes a wider hermeneutical principle. These pictures of God as transcendent

3. 1 Sam 14:41.

4. Auerbach, *Mimesis*.

reality are not arbitrary or secondary but properly indicate the most important trajectory of this faith. The seminal revelation to Moses was one example. There are others in the prophetic tradition of oracles collected in the book of Isaiah from experiences of Babylonian exile in the sixth century BC. There too the mystery, transcendence, and uniqueness of God, however experienced, is expressed even more explicitly. God is described as Lord of earth "and heaven," the everlasting Lord and Creator of all reality, not just of one tribe or people. More radically still, God is a reality beyond all normal categories, exceeding understanding: "To whom will you then liken God? . . . Have you not known? . . . It is He who sits above the circle of the earth . . . [whose] inhabitants are like grasshoppers . . . " "His ways are not our ways and His thoughts are not our thoughts."[5] It is a vision of the divine as a transcendent reality who owes his being to nothing else and cannot be compared to anything else.

Moreover, and most important, the trajectory is similar in the Christian New Testament where God appears uniquely in Christ. It is a form of revelation which is always pointing towards the transcendent and universal. For what originally appears just as a particular localized bodily form of God in Jesus is soon seen to be universalized as well. With the dramas of resurrection, Pentecost, and ascension, the localized body is transformed. It changes, then disappears altogether, then re-appears metaphorically in the collective body of his followers. It is then even more radically changed as a transcendent reality in the "heavenly realms." In this way the event of the incarnational drama as a whole reframes the meaning of the divine "body" to overcome the limitations of an over-defined localized description of bodily reality and expand the range of reference. God as a particular personal presence is now also unequivocally a non-tribal transcendent reality, knowable universally in spirit and truth not just limited to a visible human body. John's Gospel, Paul, and the writer to the Hebrews (representing some of the earliest reflective Christian thinkers) all unfold this sort of expanded meaning.

5. Cf. Isa 40:18–22; 55:8–9.

Once we see this is the decisive trajectory in Scripture its lingering literalisms and superstitions may then be reasonably stripped away, or at least relativized. What remains is a religion and religiosity incorporating the particular and personal but also always conveying a distinctive transcendent meaning. It is a trajectory which shows, in Auerbach's view, that something must have happened here that never happened in ancient Greece, or in most surrounding tribes. Something happened to the Judaeo-Christian meaning of God which, without causing it to jettison God's personal quality, cut it free from crude anthropomorphisms and marked out its transcendent distinctiveness. *What* happened is opaque. We may simply have to call it revelation, mediated through these pivotal historical moments which scriptural accounts record. But however it occurred, the key point remains that this transcendent meaning is established. Scripture's profusion of narrative and images may well be a polyphony. But it is not a cacophony. A radically transcendent meaning to the divine is core to its meaning.

God as Personal Address, Moral Reality, Personal Agency

Crucially however, this gesturing to the transcendent does not mean the divine just becomes vacuous or abstract. Far from it. A concrete, immanent, personal reality of God is still being portrayed in these Scriptures even where its overall trajectory is pushing us beyond normal language and its limits. This too is conveyed particularly through the dramatic form of much Scripture, rather than in propositions.[6] Drama can dynamically both stretch and shape the descriptions and images of the divine being offered, allowing a reference range beyond their limited propositional content but also still offering real, substantive, meaning.

Consider for example these descriptions of dramatic encounter with God:

6. There is, of course, no contradiction here. Even in the more propositional language of metaphysics which Scripture eschews, radical transcendence does not exclude or displace immanence. On the contrary, it includes it. See further below, pp. 106–10.

They heard the sound of the Lord God walking in the garden at the time of the evening breeze, and the man and his wife hid themselves from the presence of the Lord God among the trees of the garden. But the Lord God called to the man and said to him. "Where are you?" He said, "I heard the sound of you in the garden and I was afraid, because I was naked; and I hid myself."

The Lord appeared to Abraham by the oaks of Mamre, as he sat at the entrance of his tent in the heat of the day. He looked up and saw three men standing near him . . .

And the Lord descended in the cloud and stood with him there and proclaimed the name "The Lord." . . . and the Lord passed before him and proclaimed 'The Lord, the Lord, a God merciful and gracious, slow to anger and abounding in steadfast love and faithfulness."

Then the Lord answered Job out of the whirlwind: "who is this that darkens counsel by words without knowledge? Gird up your loins like a man: I will question you. . . . Where were *you* when I laid the foundations of the earth?"

'In the beginning was the Word, and the Word was with God, and the Word was God . . . and the Word became flesh and lived among us. . . . He was in the world. . . . Yet the world did not know Him.

Jesus came to Galilee, proclaiming the good news of God saying, "The time is fulfilled, the Kingdom of God has come near . . ."

During supper Jesus . . . got up from the table . . . and began to wash his disciples feet and to wipe them with the towel that was tied around him.

Now as Saul was . . . approaching Damascus, suddenly a light from heaven flashed around him. He fell to the

ground. . . . He asked "Who are you Lord?" The reply
came "I am Jesus . . ."[7]

These represent only a small sample from very different
sources, compiled over a period of more than a thousand years;
some from oral traditions of Israel's deep past relating to mythi-
cal timeless stories; some from documentary sources recounting
experiences of particular historical events; some written to help
make sense of what was happening at times of national crisis like
the Babylonian exile; some reflections from the early Christian
community as it recalled the life of Christ. But from that kaleido-
scope of contexts there is nonetheless this common texture and
outcome. They are all conveying substantive meanings of God
through this drama and dialogue of the events they recount.

What are these meanings? We still have to be wary when
specifying them. Because they refer to encounter with God they
are always still conveying the obliqueness and mystery by which
God must be imagined; they remain nuanced, reticent, metaphorically expressed. These examples reinforce the point. In the passages from the Hebrew Bible, for instance, there is a mysterious
undescribed presence walking in the cool of the garden; there is an
unresolved mirage appearing in the shimmering heat of the day, of
those three figures in one voice; there is a *veiled* appearance of God
in cloud and whirlwind; there is an *unseen* act of creation (God
is "the one who formed the earth" but when we were not there:
"where were you when I laid the foundations of the earth?"). The
pattern is similar in the New Testament passages. Where God has
"become flesh in Christ and lived among us" God was still not always clearly recognized; "He was in the world but the world did not
know him." When Saul experienced God in Christ in his dramatic
encounter he too did not know him. In Jesus's act of proclamation
in the Gospel passage there is also mystery and metaphor. God is
not simply a person but more allusively described as a "kingdom";
that is, in a set of *relationship*s (unexpected relationships in which

7. Gen 3:8–9; 18:1–2; Exod 34:5–7; Job 38:1–4; John 1:1, 14, 10; Mark
1:14–15; John 13:2, 5; Acts 9:3, 5.

God is revealed in acts not of power but of humility, service, forgiveness, washing feet).

Even so, positive and substantive meanings of God do still emerge in this oblique way. There are meanings here which go beyond merely abstract or general metaphysical attributes of God (e.g., God as ultimate "ground of being," or "final cause"). There are here specific features of God conveyed contingently in these dramas, not just abstractions. Three in particular stand out, I suggest, from these examples.

First, most notably, they consistently convey the sense that God is a personal presence. As such God is also a communicating presence. The experience of a personal presence and a communicating presence are inseparable. It is the defining mark of what Martin Buber, another Jewish philosopher, called an "I-*thou*" relationship (as distinct from "I-it"). We feel personally *addressed* when in the presence of another person, in a way we do not in the presence of an inert object like a brick or a stone. And this is the experience of God being conveyed again and again in these biblical dramas. It is the unique pull of personal communication which we receive in the presence of another personal reality. So when Saul fell to the ground he asked not *what* is this but "*who* are you, Lord?"

This does not mean God is being presented anthropomorphically after all, simply as a person like any other. It does not imply God is a bodily person whom we hear speaking as an auditory phenomenon in the way other people speak. The whole point of the obliqueness and mystery of these representations is to forbid that sort of literal, crude interpretation. So they are not experiences in which we encounter just a replica of ourselves, nor do they require that we see some other person or hear specific words. They are, rather, an experience of personal address which is always "other" than the ordinary people and events of our perception, even though often mediated through them.

This sort of experience may occur in a multitude of ways. In both the scriptural narratives and wider testimony it can supervene through almost any significant moment. It has occurred in the biblical dramas through journeys, through births, deaths, acts of hospitality and compassion, a burning bush, or just a flowering bush. In wider testimony a former Bishop of Winchester described it as being personally addressed through a flaming English sunset, glimpsed briefly on a journey out of the train window.[8] There will be countless other such examples. But the common element remains. There is a sense of a personal pull on us, addressing us. It comes not just from the events of the world around us but also through them, from a personal presence beyond them as well as within them. And that personal address is a primary feature of what God means.

The second feature is that these personal encounters also have a specifically moral nature. In other words, this experience of being addressed by God is not just a perception of a general, shapeless, spiritual reality; it is the perception of a personal presence with a determinate nature. It is the perception of a reality with a mind and will who has particular views about things, who wills one thing and not another. So for instance, in the garden experience, Adam reacts to God not just as the general ground of his being but as one who has given him a sense of value and specific moral choice. Or at Sinai, Moses is being shown a specific moral character of God passing before him out of the cloud, a God of steadfast love and faithfulness. Then pre-eminently, in the drama of Christ's life, God is made known in a specific kingdom of moral relationships, a particular way of living together which he lived and taught in the parables of the kingdom (the way of hospitality, justice, generosity, forgiveness).

This is not the same as saying God meets us in a specific moral code or detailed set of moral rules. Biblical texts certainly describe how cultures and individuals formulated specific codes in response to their experiences of God. These have proved more or less useful depending on time and context, and some like the Ten Commandments have been especially enduring and authoritative. But that is not the heart of what is being conveyed in these dramas. Instead, in meeting God we are meeting something more

8. Taylor, *Go-Between God*.

fundamental than a contingent set of rules; we are meeting the source of all value, the meaning of goodness itself. God in these dramatic encounters is the reality which gives ultimate reason to all value, the reality whose creation of things makes things matter at all. God is that which gives a value to things and people which is not just rooted in the utility of pleasure, security, or survival but in a moral quality derived from an ultimate source in the eternal God. This is most clearly (albeit symbolically) expressed in the Genesis myth where God is described creating the world as good, then putting the tree of the knowledge of good and evil in the garden to show he is the ultimate source of this goodness and value. All moral choices which follow are made moral by that eternal divine moral origin. The pre-eminent expression of this is given in Christ when his person and life is presented as *the* way, truth and life.

Again it is important to be clear what this does not mean. It does not mean that a sense of meeting ultimate value and goodness entails believing in a universal content to morality, any more than it entails specific rules. It is the *form* of the moral demand which has this sense of ultimacy and absolute authority, not its content which may be relative to context. Nor does it mean that moral experience itself entails belief in God, logically or psychologically. A sense of absolute and authoritative moral claim and ultimate value is widespread, with or without religious faith.[9] Anyone may experience it whether or not they call it God. Immanuel Kant recognized this in what he called the a priori moral sense and the categorical imperative which arises from it.

The chief point, however, is simply that this sense of absolute moral authority does as a matter of fact belong to the essential meaning of God presented in these scriptural dramas (irrespective of our actual belief in God). And this is surely what we might expect. It is the fact that this personal presence who addresses us is essentially *moral* which gives the experience its unique authority. It also helps explain how and why this sort of religious experience, in some form, is so widespread. It is precisely because it coincides so closely with the experience of value and morality. As atheist

9. See discussion of this in previous chapter, "Meanings of Morality."

philosopher Simon Critchley found, an experience of ultimate value is almost exactly like the compelling pull we experience when meeting an extraordinarily strong and attractive personality—it is both a personal and "god-like" summons.[10] And the point here is simply that the moral claim is like God because God *is* moral reality. This is what God actually *means* in the biblical dramas.

The final and equally inescapable feature of God is simply the sense of agency. As the narratives unfold we consistently see God *active*. God brings people out of one place into another, from the garden to the desert to Gethsemane; God forgives, washes feet, transforms, brings about new states of affairs (the kingdom). In other words, this moral and personal reality is not just an ultimate origin of things and their value but also a mover of things. God is not just a personal communicating presence but a personal agent who does things, makes things happen. The divine reality of these dramas has causal power. This too fits with the perception that God is personal. It is, after all, part of the normal definition of a personal reality to have an effect, not to be inert. Personhood *is* agency.

What does this agency itself mean? How God carries out this agency is not straightforward. Yet we can see some patterns in the biblical dramas. Not least, to begin with, it appears to be primarily by the power of communication. When we sense ourselves addressed by God (God "speaking"), the experience has causal power. God makes things happen ("acts") in some measure simply by "speaking," making his mind and will known. We can think of this by human analogy. Even finite human agents have an effect when they communicate their mind and will. We do this daily. We add information into the world by expressing our mind and this is never neutral; it has an effect. It changes how other people act. The moment we share our thoughts with someone else they react in some way, however marginally or imperceptibly, whether consciously or unconsciously.

We could venture further analogies. Quantum mechanics now also suggests that at the subatomic level change is brought about just by the mind's observation, even without intentional

10. As noted in previous chapter. Cf. Critchley, *Infinitely Demanding*.

communication with another. But we do not have to understand quantum mechanics to see the more general point about the mind's causal effect. Move from the subatomic level to the larger field of human history and this becomes particularly visible. A twentieth-century historian, commenting on Hitler's Germany, offers a fascinating if chilling example.[11] He points out that much of the collective action of the Third Reich came about simply because Hitler made his mind and will known. Hitler did not do much directly, and did not always make his mind known in proactive ways by giving specific orders. On the contrary he often conveyed his views only in general ways. But that was enough. Just that input of information was sufficient for henchmen to pursue their policies because they felt they were (in the historian's sinister phrase) "working towards the Fuhrer," "working towards the mind of Hitler." So replace a malign human dictator's mind with a moral divine mind and we have another analogy of one way in which the God of these biblical narratives acts. In many and varied ways God is making the divine mind known so that we can work towards it.

This lies at the heart of almost all the dramas and dialogues throughout the biblical narratives. The divine mind is being made known precisely through this multitude of events and persons, and then pre-eminently in Christ. As a consequence, the characters of the Bible from Abraham and Moses to Jesus's disciples are all variously (and of course imperfectly) "working towards God's mind." Likewise, all others who experience the mind of God anonymously addressing them in the rest of human history are also contributing. In this way the kingdom of God is unfolded, and a transcendent divine causal power is continually being exercised. It may appear to happen only sporadically and sometimes only at glacial pace; it often appears frustrated and abused by the freedom and contingency of the human world through which God acts; but it is occurring nonetheless.

We could also extend the analogy by drawing from the human creative process of authorship. We might imagine God's agency in the human world as analogous to the way an author or playwright

---

11. Kershaw, "Working Towards the Führer."

steers her literary work, both in detail and in its overall shape and outcome. Authors can do this because they radically transcend their work in a similar way to God's transcendence of this world. They exist in a different category of reality which transcends the time and space of the work itself. And it is from that metaphysically distinct vantage point that the author can operate a constant communicative interaction with the characters who all "work towards the mind of the author"—without denying the integrity of each actor in their own space and time.

God is represented acting in other ways too. The scriptural snapshots of drama cited also include verbs of more direct action, not just indirect communicative action. God "walks" as well as "talks"; God "comes, passes by, lays the foundations of the world"; God "became flesh and lived among us"; God healed the sick and stilled storms. As with all talk of God we must take these as metaphorical statements. But the point is that even as metaphors these convey more than just a divine action of dialogue, more than an action of mind to mind. They also seem to portray divine (inter) action more directly as a form of agency within the structures of the wider physical world, not just within human consciousness.

How this kind of agency might be understood is again not easy. So for example, to conceive this divine action bringing about, or preventing, an occurrence simply by replacing natural causes with a divine cause cannot possibly be plausible. That kind of supernatural intervention would raise too many unanswerable questions. There are the familiar, devastating moral questions which God would face. For if that is how God acts, why are the natural causes which bring cancer, dementia, earthquakes not more often replaced? There are also the fundamental theological questions already touched on. To imagine God acting in the physical world like that reduces God's causality to the same sort of thing as any other natural cause. That is theologically unthinkable, as well as empirically without foundation, because it reduces God to anthropomorphic dimensions—which is precisely what Scripture for the most part refuses to do. God cannot be reduced to the nature of other realities within the universe otherwise God would not be *God*, a radically transcendent reality.

But it is not impossible to conceive it in other ways. What it requires is the imagining of a different kind of causation altogether. Divine agency must be imagined working patiently and invisibly, steering events through the natural web of things, rather than by replacing them. This is conceptually challenging, but congruent with the meaning of God as a radically transcendent reality. Since God is not just an instance of a kind which can be compared to others, God's causality must also be construed in this way. It will be of a wholly different order. It cannot be thought of as an additional cause showing up empirically alongside other causal chains, or competing with them. Instead it will be conceivable precisely as a causality which works without displacing other causes, without requiring gaps in other causal accounts, without showing up on our ordinary empirical radar.

One analogy which now presents itself to support this sort of picture derives from information technology. Science now sometimes describes natural events operating according to an input of "information" into the world processes at subatomic level, not unlike the way a software program operates within the hardware of a computer, affecting everything that happens. So we could now conceive transcendent divine action in the world (natural as well as human) to be like this constant hidden input of information. Its "causality," like that of software, is of a different order to the spatio-temporal hardware of the material universe. In this way it can be imagined operating invisibly at every point in and through natural processes and contingencies, affecting outcomes but without disrupting the processes.

Whether or not these analogies satisfy, however, the overall point remains. God as conveyed through the drama and dialogues of the Hebrew-Christian Scriptures undoubtedly has agency. It is an essential further part of what God means, and inseparable from the other features of God as personal and moral address. And taken together these surely now provide a real basis for meaning. They offer some definite, even if not definitive, meaning overall.

God is by no means without substantive shape or content just because transcendent. Yes, the important parameters must still operate. God is not to be anthropomorphically conceived, not to be imagined literally as a person whose being and acting replicates ours. God is describable only in metaphor. Nonetheless, given these parameters, God can still be described. God is a personal, communicating, relational presence. God is a moral reality whose creation of things and relationships gives value to them, makes them matter. God is also personal agent, a causal reality who really makes things happen. These are the foundational images for the meaning of God that the scriptural narratives consistently offer.

Transcendence and Perfection: Meanings of God in Classical Orthodoxy and Modernity

Foundations, however, need to be built on. If meaning is to be credibly maintained through time and change these notions of divine personhood, agency and transcendence will always have to make sense in new interpretative frameworks, requiring new language or imagery. Even this preliminary basic exposition had to draw on some contemporary literary and scientific analogies just to establish a core meaning. So for continuing credibility, more will certainly be required.

In particular there has to be more reflection on the *juxtaposition* of the concepts and images which have emerged. The core categories of transcendence and personhood present the greatest challenge. How can we sensibly and credibly continue to affirm a truly transcendent God *and* a truly personal God? Both have emerged as essential ingredients in the meaning of divinity. But how are they compatible? This conundrum has long lain at the heart of Western theological reflection. If God means both, does this stretch meaning to breaking point? Or does it enrich meaning and bolster credibility? The struggle to make sense of both, and the creative dialogue between them, is central to the quest for meaning. There is a long story of theological reflection turning on this which needs exploration.

Instincts for Perfection

Critical to this story, I suggest, is first more understanding about transcendence, and the hold it has exercised over us. Transcendence is less accessible than notions of personhood and agency. Yet its grip on the theological imagination is incontrovertible. So it needs more justification and explication. This in turn means seeing how it emerged not just within Scripture itself but from another source altogether, the Athenian philosopher Plato who lived in the fourth and fifth centuries BC.

Plato's background lay in the anthropomorphic warring figures who populated his fellow Greeks' religion. These Homeric gods made little sense to him. They were only constructed fables. They were immoral, irrational, superstitions which did not exist as ultimate realities at all. So to grasp ultimate reality more truly Plato needed to look beyond and behind these passing human projections. But he did not do this on the basis of particular prophetic religious experiences or from particular historical events of revelation as Hebraic-Christian faith supposes, nor by observation and sense experience as modern scientific method supposes. Instead his view emerged from reason combined with what might be called intellectual intuition; a kind of reasoned mysticism. In this view what appears most real—the world of visible and tangible things, bricks and bodies, planets and plants—is only a passing appearance since these things all ultimately fade and decay. There must be instead some necessary, eternal, and perfect reality lying beyond or behind these transient and finite appearances. He used a celebrated allegory to help make his point.[12] The ordinary visible reality which passes in front of us is only like shadows on a cave wall lit by a fire. If we could see outside the cave we would realize that this is not the whole of reality, nor ultimate reality. Only outside in the sun do we see the lasting world, and realize that our experience in the cave is just passing smoke and mirrors.

12. There are multiple and sometimes contested interpretations of this allegory, political and educational, as well as metaphysical.

We should not underestimate the force of this intuition that things of ordinary time and change are not ultimate but depend on something eternal and unchanging (something more like the truths of mathematics). It is not just a premodern intuition we find in Plato. It also resonates with some elements of current science and mathematical physics. Here there are similar suggestions which suggest that time is not an absolute, ordinary matter is not ultimate but dissolves into energy, and the ultimate structures of reality are timelessly ordered more like mathematical forms. It resonates too with existential concerns, in any age. It lies behind ideas of ourselves as people with an eternal soul, the intuition that the real essence of ourselves is not the appearance of our present changing bodies but some potentially eternal self or soul lying behind or within them; an instinct that here in this world we are not yet fully ourselves or fully at home.

The chief point here, however, is how readily this instinct also transfers specifically to God. It marks out a unique meaning of God, both conceptually and as an object of worship. God by this definition means precisely this reality lying behind time and change. God means a reality which is absolute, eternal, perfect, necessary, complete, without change, decay, imperfection. For Christian theologians the notions of divine transcendence and resistance to anthropomorphism found in the Hebraic origins of faith provide a natural warrant for this. As we saw, these Hebraic roots typically use narrative form and personal encounter rather than propositional or abstract reasoning to express this aspect of divinity. But the fundamental intuition is much the same. If God is Lord and Creator of the whole universe, rather than simply part of it, God must indeed be a radically different order of being and existence to the rest of reality.

Small wonder, then, that many theologians of classical orthodox Christian faith reflected this fundamentally platonic idea generally in their doctrine of God. They also developed it. They unfolded this transcendent meaning in specific attributes of God, to give some formal shape to the intuition.[13] There is what is called

13. Most notably, and seminally, expounded by the medieval theologian Thomas Aquinas in his *Summa Theologica*.

the "simplicity" of God (God cannot be divided up into different parts as ordinary spatial, temporal life is); the "necessity" of God (God depends on nothing in order to be, God cannot not exist but necessarily exists, like the truths of mathematics); the "aseity" of God (God is wholly complete, self-sufficient, actualized, with no unrealized potential which would imply incompleteness or imperfection); the "eternity" of God (God is beyond time); the "immutability" of God (God is beyond change); and the "impassibility" of God (God is beyond suffering).

Moreover, these meanings of God have not been just the preserve of formal theology. They also became deeply embedded in the articles of church faith, and in liturgy. The thirty-nine articles of the Church of England, for example, refer to "One God . . . without body, parts, or passion." The collect (prayer) for Trinity Sunday invites us to acknowledge the glory of the *eternal* Trinity. Christian hymnody has also incorporated much of it in its imagery. A familiar hymn tells us that God is "Immortal, Invisible" in "light inaccessible" (the light beyond Plato's cave, perhaps). God is "unresting, unhasting, neither wanting, nor wasting . . ." We may "blossom and flourish as leaves on the tree/ And wither and perish . . . but nought changeth thee." In another hymn, "Change and decay all around I see. *O Thou who changest not*, abide with me." "Heaven's morning breaks and earth's vain shadows flee. . . . In life, in death, O Lord abide with me" (the shadows here again surely referencing Plato's cave). The power of these images is unsurprising when we realize how profoundly they are offering existential reassurance, not just concepts to engage the mind. The insistence that this passing world does not have the final word, this doctrine of radical transcendence, is clearly not just an abstraction for the intellect but also feeding the soul.

Transcendence *and* Personhood

This background to the radical transcendence of God helps unfold at least some its meaning. But of course it also sharpens that abiding question for theology we identified. It helps demonstrate why there is such an acute issue of *coherence* if the wider range of personal images for God is also brought into play. How can this unchanging, complete, timeless perfection of transcendent divine reality coexist with a truly personal divine nature? Personal reality, after all, is normally characterized as intrinsically and reciprocally relational, fluid, dynamic. It is constituted essentially as relational by a wider world of other persons and processes which itself is also responsive, dynamic, changing. Personhood in this world (and especially love) is therefore inseparable from time, change, even suffering. How then can a God beyond time and change be considered truly personal? A *"thou"* who *"changest not"* appears to be a contradiction in terms. How can God be a real "thou," yet also as eternal and unchanging as mathematics? In short, it seems that when ideas of an eternal reality of absolute being are juxtaposed with the image of a personal moral presence who responds, speaks, and acts, there is a conflation of contradictory images as problematic as the grinding of two tectonic plates. It was not a problem for Plato because his notion of ultimate reality was not this kind of personal God. But if the ultimate *is* personal the problem presses, apparently intractably.

This conundrum appears all through Christian faith and practice. It is evident in hymnody and liturgy, as noted. It is also intrinsic to the doctrine of Trinity, sometimes considered as the most defining Christian image of God. The idea or image of God as the three "persons," yet one reality, expresses both the personal form of God *and* a form of being and existence transcending any personal reality we know. As Father, Son, and Spirit God is imagined as a dynamic personal relationship of love within God's own being, played out historically in Christ as a relationship with his Father into which he was drawn by the Spirit. But equally it implies radical transcendence of these sorts of personal categories because it is conceived as an eternal threefold relationship subsisting as one personal reality, suggesting a different category of being to anything we know. In this way Trinity expresses personhood and transcendence; but it does *not* explain them. The apparent contradictions at the heart of theism remains unresolved. It is a major issue in imagining any credible personal God.

How then has theology dealt with this? One response has been to drop or downplay one side or the other of the paradox in oscillation, one side dominating the other. So in the history of theology at first transcendence won out. It trumped the personalist view of God. The church's classical theological tradition, at least formally, ruled out the idea that God in any way embraces growth and change in his/her own being, however essential change might seem to personhood. One reason for this was the strong influence of Greek metaphysics already noted. The notion that ultimate reality must be beyond all time, change, and suffering, was simply considered non-negotiable if God is really to be *God*. And while it could be granted that God suffered and changed in the temporal human nature of Christ, this was not countenanced for God as ultimate reality, God in God's own eternal being. Instead "patripassianism," the view that God the Father suffers and changes, was explicitly deemed a heresy. This persisted through much formal theology even into modernity—whatever popular piety has thought or felt.

But then the oscillation. Much contemporary Western theology has now reversed this. Theology has predominantly opted for the other side of the conundrum. It has prioritized personal images for God, with all the implications this carries. God more recently has been conceived primarily within the experience of time, change, and even suffering. The shift has been so wholesale that it has now effectively become a heresy to say God does *not* suffer or change. Discussions about the haunting issue of theodicy (whether any meaning of God could ever be "justified" in the light of great evil and suffering) illustrate the shift starkly. In order to deal with our suffering it is now widely assumed that God *must* him/herself suffer and change. And this is presented with the same sense of theological and intuitive certainty that the platonically inspired classic theologians had insisted for its opposite (i.e., that the consoling God must be beyond all suffering and change).

There are various reasons for the shift. In part it is because of the way science has displaced, or changed, metaphysics. Some (though not all) scientific analyses of the nature of reality increasingly suggested that the ultimate stuff of the universe is nothing but flux, change, process. It then becomes harder to see what basis there could be for metaphysics to propose any ultimate reality beyond such flux. The particular metaphysics of radical transcendence has also been further critiqued from within philosophy itself.[14] There are also more specifically theological reasons. There has been re-awakened interest in those elements of trinitarian theology which had always stressed the being of God as primarily and essentially a personal web of relationships with nothing "beyond" (a possible Cappadocian reading from the fourth century). There has also been a revival of interest in those Hebraic roots of biblical theology which appear to foreground personal and dynamic images of God to such an extent that its elements of radical metaphysical transcendence are easily sidelined. They have been dismissed as illegitimate anachronisms or just alien intrusions of Greek metaphysics, rather than intrinsic and legitimate elements of the biblical views.

But perhaps the chief reason for the shift, acting cumulatively with these others, has been the effect of the sheer scale of suffering of twentieth century, especially the Holocaust. Great evil and suffering did not begin in the last century of course, but the world has become more conscious of it, and the consequences for theology are evident. If God is believed at all then, as already indicated, this has been taken to mean that God must now be conceived in him/herself to be suffering with us. Dietrich Bonhoeffer, the Lutheran pastor-theologian killed for resisting Hitler, famously stated this explicitly. He came to believe that only a God who himself really suffers and changes can be a truly credible God for us in *our* suffering and change; "only a suffering God can help," he wrote from prison.[15]

For all these reasons, then, this later theological trajectory has been notable and not much challenged in recent decades.

14. See further on this below, pp. 107–8.

15. Bonhoeffer, *Letters and Papers from Prison*, 197.

Personalist images of God have largely held sway, transcendence has been "domesticated,"[16] and images from classical orthodoxy of a God beyond change and suffering have often been left only in the *cul de sacs* of our religious history. This is reckoned to fit better with the wider temper of our age, and it certainly eases the ancient conundrum about coherence in our meaning of God.

Even so tides do turn again. Earlier views rarely disappear entirely but re-emerge, even if differently framed. So in fact the oscillation continues.[17] And this is hardly surprising bearing in mind the full range of foundational images of Scripture. Those radically transcendent images for the divine remain. They cannot so easily be domesticated or discarded. Images of the inscrutable God of Isaiah's vision, maker of heaven and earth but not part of it, and the Almighty God beyond the suffering Christ as well as within him, are too deeply embedded in Scripture to be jettisoned just as Greek intrusion. Likewise, the ancient instinct for absolutes which moved past philosophers and poets persists. So even though it has had to engage with evolutionary science, the new physics of process, and the experiences of twentieth-century suffering, radical transcendence has not disappeared. Our twentieth-century poetic high priests are eloquent witnesses to this, as much as formal theology. In the midst of war T. S. Eliot for example reached again for images of ultimate metaphysical unity, a state *beyond* time and passion. His final quartet *Little Gidding* is a telling expression of this. Set against the backdrop of the blitz in London, it is a sustained attempt to find images for an ultimate meaning behind the immediate experience and restless polarities of change and lost time which assailed him through the falling of bombs and the fires. In one terrible, almost blasphemous, image Eliot describes a falling bomb in terms of the transcendent fire of the Holy Spirit. For him our current experience of chaos, entropy, and the destruction of time, is not final. It masks something beyond the fractured tyrannies of time, both future and

---

16. A phrase used by Placher, *Domestication of Transcendence*.

17. Signs of this appear to range from a modest revival in neo-Thomist classical theology, to feminist and liberationist critiques of a relational God himself/herself too powerless to help the powerless.

the past. God is not explicitly specified in that poem, but God is in mind, precisely as an absolute and eternal God.

The specific, devastating, issue of suffering can sometimes now play a contrary role in this further twist to the story. Some theologians now see a continued necessity of metaphysical absolutes in God *because of* evil and suffering, not in spite of them. Where Bonhoeffer's experience of suffering led him to believe God is able to help only if God too suffers, others have found the opposite. Theologian Frances Young, for example, offers a surprising theological reflection after the birth of her severely handicapped son and the sacrificial experience of bringing him up. As a theologian of the late twentieth century she might have been expected to reach exclusively for the prevailing view that only a personal suffering God would make sense of her situation—if any sense can be made at all. But in fact the image of God which connected most deeply with her was the opposite. A God who is only with us in the terms and experience of this life, however empathetic, is precisely the one who *cannot* help enough because God's capacity to help is compromised by God's total involvement. As we are only helped out of a hole by someone reaching us from outside (not just in it with us) so we are helped in our suffering by God's metaphysical foothold in eternity beyond passion and suffering (not just in it with us).

In short, the oscillation continues unresolved. Neither radically transcendent nor personalist meanings of God seem to be sufficient on their own. And so it is that some of the most creative moves reject a binary approach altogether, trying instead to retain elements of the classical metaphysics of the patristic and medieval writers *alongside* more personal Hebraic categories, however challenging the juxtaposition remains. Young herself provides one example. Speaking reflectively from her own particular experience again, she puts it like this: "From that experience I found myself reclaiming the insight that God is beyond suffering . . . at the same time in Christ he subjected himself to personal involvement in pain and anguish . . . the two ideas somehow belong together . . . and our knowledge of God is impoverished if we cannot stretch our minds and imaginations to encompass both."[18] This, it seems, offers less of an oscillation between two sides of a paradox, more an attempt to embrace both. It suggests that living with apparent contradiction may in the end be a more credible way to do full justice to the mystery of the meaning of God than resolving it. In the pursuit of meaning, transcendence and personhood will both have to remain equally in our imagination even though it continues to stretch our reason.

Struggling with Paradox

It has to be said that Western theology does not easily acquiesce in this because of its instincts for conceptual coherence. But it has sometimes tried. To reconcile the conundrum a metaphysical movement called process theology has attempted, for example, to conceive God with two poles or aspects both essentially constituting God's being. God is imagined with both a concrete and an absolute pole. This permits us to think of time, change, responsiveness, suffering occurring within the concrete pole of God's being without limiting God, because God's absolute being remains "intact." It allows change and time to occur within God without overwhelming or wholly defining God in the way they do with us.

Alternatively, there have been attempts to reconcile these polarities by using the discourses of science more than metaphysics. Physics, for example, can offer new models to help combine contrasting concepts when imagining divine action in the world. I have already touched on this. If divine action is conceived as something like an input of "information" at the subatomic level, this sets the conditions of our natural systems rather like a computer program determines processes. In this way God can be conceived as constantly and effectively interacting with a changing world, through its indeterminacies, while operating through a wholly "other" transcendent form of causation. Alternatively divine action can be conceived less as an input of information at subatomic

18. Young, *Face to Face*, 239.

level and more top down on the world systems as a whole—rather as a mind might work through its body. Again, this offers a picture of how the divine mind is transcendent, a different order of being and causation, but still effectively and personally affecting a temporal world.[19]

Do these attempts succeed? Not wholly. They all leave some issues unresolved. Process metaphysics too easily reduces the absolute pole of God merely to abstraction. Scientific discourses are too prone to revision to provide secure analogies. The *whole* meaning of God, it seems, still continues to resist either conceptual tidiness or precise, stable analogies. Trying to fit God into any verbal or conceptual formula is (in novelist Dorothy Sayers's homely image) like trying to force a large and irritated cat into a small basket: as soon as you tuck in his head, his tail comes out; once his back paws are inside, the front paws appear again; when you finally manage to squeeze the cat into the basket his wails within make it perfectly clear you have only succeeded anyway by violating something in its essential being and dignity.[20] And so for all this further reflection on core images of God at least some paradox remains, the struggle for coherence is never entirely won, and the conundrums that divine reality has generated are rarely if ever resolved.

Yet does this matter? It is not that theology has considered the concept or experience of God and simply cried "mystery." It is still an attempt to wrestle meaning out of the mysteries of paradox, so it is not an abdication of the quest for meaning altogether. If anything it just broadens the scope, stimulating further attempts to hold together these apparent contradictions as a potential source of further meaning. The very process of discovering how difficult it is to convey God with clear, consistent and coherent concepts may lead us to explore meanings beyond our finite, limited, resolved categories of reasoned experience—and isn't that actually a more plausible outcome for the meaning of God? Must not "God," by definition, embrace just that sort of unconfined meaning? A tidier God might be wanted but in the end an unconfined God of

19. To follow up this discussion, see Yong, "Divining 'Divine Action.'"
20. Dorothy Sayers, quoted in McGrath, *Faith and the Creeds*.

Scripture and further tradition is surely going to be more credible just because s/he will *not* fit, even with the most strenuous efforts.

In short, if we find we have to leave apparently contradictory images of God playing alongside each other, the quest for both meaning and credibility may be enhanced not diminished. God is perfect, eternal, unchanging. God is also personal, active, changing. Yes, this stretches reason. But might not the apparent contradiction actually reflect reality more truly?

Mystery and Play: Meanings of God in Mysticism and Postmodernity

In fact this use of paradox as a further authentic source of meaning has always been part of Christian history in a number of different ways. It was a major ingredient of pre-modern mysticism. It is also apparent in devotional and poetic literature where reason and imagination coalesce more easily. Now more recently it has been positively embraced within the pluralism of postmodernity, which feeds off all these sources. And so perhaps these offer an apt final lens. Can we now pursue the (paradoxical) meanings of God even further through these mystical, imaginative, and postmodern traditions? How does meaning develop when mysticism, mystery, and imagination are intentionally given fuller rein in these ways? How, if at all, might they add to the meanings of scriptural and classical foundations? Again, a wide terrain to cover which I can only touch on selectively. Yet surely fertile ground to plough.

Early Mysticism: Desire, Negation, Abundance, Mystery

To begin with the early mystical traditions, these offer a context for paradox pre-eminently in their distinctive *experience* of God. It was characteristically an experience of intense yearning and desire. The meaning of God emerges through our yearning for God. Its nearest approximation is *eros*, an experience of extraordinary attraction which draws two persons together. So for the mystics

"God" means the kind of reality which elicits intense desire, and experience of God is pre-eminently a desire to contemplate and be united with the desired. Within this experience the mystics encountered profound mystery but were also drawn further into the mystery by their desire so that desire became a kind of knowing, notwithstanding the mystery. In this way yearning and love is considered a pathway to real knowledge of God. Rational concepts are insufficient. Saint Augustine was one of the earliest reflective writers to express this in a systematic way. God is the kind of reality who is known through love as much as through the intellect (which itself only operates effectively through love). Only through the union of love are we fully and reliably in touch with truth, and with meaning.

As with classical orthodoxy, this too follows some contours of platonic philosophy. Plato taught that it is part of the very structure of reality that our souls must yearn to ascend their eternal source and be united to it, because that is their true home. But platonism is by no means the only or primary source. The pattern is also found in Scripture. It is apparent in the psalms of yearning ("as a deer longs for flowing streams").[21] It is expressed memorably in The Song of Songs where human erotic love is used as the image ("my beloved thrust his hand into the opening and my inmost being yearned for him").[22] In the New Testament Paul longs to be united with Christ, to share his life and even his suffering. John's Gospel speaks of abiding in Christ, using images of deep union with him (we are to be as "branches joined to a vine").[23] Unsurprisingly, then, the early mystics found meditation specifically on Scripture to be a significant catalyst for their new experiences and new meanings. Early church fathers such as Clement (150–ca. 215), Origen (ca. 185–ca. 254), and then Saint Augustine himself (354–430) all approached God in this way, as did the earlier Jewish philosopher Philo.

21. Ps 42:1.
22. Song 5:4–6.
23. See John 15:1–5.

But what then are the specific images of God which emerge from these experiences? They are varied, elusive, and certainly paradoxical. But they still yield meaning. One of most generative accounts is presented in the fifth- or early sixth-century writings of a figure who himself, perhaps suitably, remains shrouded in mystery (Pseudo-Dionysius).[24] He describes being led up "beyond the unknowing and light, up to the farthest, highest, peak of mystic Scripture, where the mysteries of God's Word lie . . . simple, absolute, and unchangeable . . . in the brilliant darkness of a hidden silence." Personal desire is drawing him in this experience, and to that extent God is known as personal. Yet what he is perceiving is not simply another person but something beyond ordinary personhood, something "simple, absolute, and unchangeable." The personal images are here transcended by impersonal. But then these too are themselves transcended. He is also led "beyond light," and further (oxymoronically) to a "brilliant darkness." In another passage we are invited to "to leave behind everything perceived and understood . . . all that is and is not," because if "with your understanding laid aside you strive . . . towards union with Him," you will meet one "beyond all being and knowledge." Here again it seems we are first approaching a "Him" (a personal reality, something knowable in personal terms), yet "He" is also known as unknown and inexpressible, "beyond all being and knowledge."[25]

In short, these experiences offer numerous positive images but also seem to deny or radically qualify them. God is personal being but also beyond all being. God is a brilliance but also darkness. This is a pattern of much mystical theology. Whatever is affirmed of God is also denied, or transcended. The effect is never to allow us to settle in any one picture. We are always being moved on to something other and greater, beyond anything we can grasp.

Is this restless appeal to different and even contradictory images just perverse and irrational? Not necessarily. First, it is important simply as a record of what emerges from the fullness of the experience itself. If we are to be true to the experience then we

24. Pseudo-Dionysius, *Mystical Theology*.
25. Pseudo-Dionysius, *Mystical Theology* 1.1, 1.2.

should not prematurely close down aspects of it just for the sake of coherence. But it is also important to see the deeper rationality of the apparent incoherence, not just to record it. By declining to settle on only one image or compatible set of images these expressions of faith are refusing to reduce the meaning of God only to one kind of thing in our experience. Far from irrationality this is a rational response to transcendence. It is reminding us that a God who is beyond all these things cannot be fully expressed by them. It is displaying the deeper rationality of transcendence and of infinity; apparently contradictory descriptions may be the only way to make sense of an infinite reality.

It seems likely that this is what Pseudo-Dionysius himself believed he was doing. He was conveying meaning by a kind of infinite regress (or progress) of affirmation and denial. On the one hand because God is the infinite source of all things of this world it makes sense to offer images derived from the known things of this world to describe God, so we rightly use images like light, love, person, mind, and so on. On the other hand because God is the transcendent source of all things who cannot therefore be just like any one thing, it also makes sense to deny these images lest they limit and reduce God. But then we cannot just deny them either, for that too would also limit God. This leads to more affirmations—and so to a counterpoint of constant affirmation and denial. Thus: "since [God] surpasses all being . . . we should negate all these affirmations." Yet "the negations are not simply the opposites of the affirmations for [as] the cause of all things [God] is [also] beyond every denial."[26] In the face of the mystery which generates this sort of paradoxical response we could simply fall silent (the apophatic way). As Wittgenstein famously said 1,500 years later, "whereof one cannot speak one must be silent." This is in effect what the mystics are doing in their denials when they describe what God is *not*. But since silence and negation, on their own, also fail to do justice to the fullness of the experience of God there is also the turn to an abundance of images, not just negation. Both are necessary, and they must be taken together.

26. Pseudo-Dionysius, *Mystical Theology* 1.1, 1.2.

The critical point to reinforce here is that this dialectic of negation and affirmation is not only a necessary and fitting response to God, it really may be conveying further meaning. To say God is both light and darkness, both personal and unchanging, both three and one, is to convey something about God which can be expressed in no other way. Its effect is like that of a multi-dimensional reading of a comprehensive *curriculum vitae*, a full record of someone's life, character, and achievements. To read it merely linearly and diachronically, first one aspect followed by another, yields only a limited picture. To read it synchronically, taking it as a whole including the dynamic tension between different aspects of the same person, will reveal more of the person's true nature. Use both together and even more emerges. This is what the mystics were doing in relation to God. Drawn by their experience of intense love and longing, and following the deeper rationality of transcendence, they accepted that the structure of infinite reality of God cannot be confined in any one form of expression. The "biography" of the divine includes temporal images and eternal attributes in dialectic, apparent opposites actively playing on each other.

What then, if anything, has this mystical approach added? We could say it is only making explicit what is implicit in biblical theology and later more reflective theology. As we have seen Scripture itself offers a similar dialectical approach. It sometimes employs the *via negativa* (i.e., saying what God is not) and has marked reticence about using definite pictures of God (we can only see God's "backside"). It also employs an abundance and riot of positive contradictory images (God is Father and Son, King and servant, light and love, unchanging and responsive). The survey of later reflective theology showed something similar. It has doctrines of God who is both beyond time and change and intimately involved with it; it has its incarnational doctrines of a God who is both "without body, parts or passions" and embodied in the world with us. Yet there is a difference. This lies, I suggest, in the way mystical theology does not just state these paradoxes but celebrates them. It does not just use them as an expression of divine mystery but as a substantive exploration of it. It actively endorses them to subvert our shallow binary distinctions which so limit God (and perhaps ourselves too) and to positively enrich the meaning of God in the process.

To be sure, this does not convince all. For some the contradiction of images is just irrationality and the *via negativa* is just vacuous. The suspicion is that this is all nonsense. There is nothing real being conveyed, and no real meaning.[27] But it is clear that the mystics themselves believed they were expressing something real. Their profusion of images, contradictions, and silences, even their sense of the absence of God, were not driven by a sense of nothingness but of plenitude.[28] Their encounters with God and consequent images of God were unverifiable because they were of no thing like any other, but they were not of nothing.

The Logic of Mysticism in Modernity: Snapshots from Science and Poetry

It is also clear that this approach is not just a special pleading of pre-modern thinking about God. Something similar can be found in every age and in other fields of enquiry. Finding meaning through the denial of any one image, and the dialectic of multiple images, has survived the binary rationality of enlightenment, empiricism, positivism and early modern science, and now appears in new guises in late-modernity. It seems that there are always experiences and realities in life which will not reduce to binary formulae or empirically testable data, but which generate multiple images to reflect a greater meaning. The natural sciences undoubtedly approach the mystery of the cosmos in this way. The Cern laboratory near Geneva, for example, pursues realities at the subatomic level which defy ordinary observation so has to describe some particles in their apparent absence, just by their effects. It is a kind of *via negativa*. Realities are also often modeled by multiple positive images, even if some seem contradictory. The most celebrated is light

27. That is how Don Cupitt read the later Medieval mystic Meister Eckhart, implying he wasn't experiencing the deeper rationality of a real mystery, he was experiencing nothing meaningful at all. See Cupitt, *Taking Leave of God*.

28. Cf. Turner, *Darkness of God*.

itself which cannot be fully described in one image but is better imaged as both wave and particle. The recourse to a variety of apparently contradictory images in order to do full justice to reality relates here to a very different field of enquiry. The "objects" of scientific enquiry are very different from that of theology. But the method is at least analogous.

This approach is also evident in attempts to express more quotidian mysteries. Consider the reality of other people. We may largely take them for granted, assuming at least an overall similarity to ourselves. But in fact our ordinary experience of others' personhood is often opaque, paradoxical, fraught with apparent contradictions. To do justice to them we find we have to accept the contradictions, not reduce or rationalize them. Even the apparently simple relationship of romantic love generates a view of the other which defies easy description; the meaning of the other emerges only through a profusion of images.

Here it is poetry rather than science which best exemplifies the approach. We do not have to go further than Shakespeare's most famous sonnet. How can he describe his beloved? "Shall I compare thee to a summer's day?" *No!* "Thou art *more* lovely . . ."[29] There is the negation. But then also, *yes!* "thy eternal summer shall not fade." But still not enough. It needs qualification. It is an *eternal* summer. Then he needs further images so a further denial and other new images follow as well. Yet the outcome is not just confusion but, precisely, a new meaning which emerges in this process. Meaning is both deepened and expanded when we read the poem as a whole. Poetry generally has adopted this approach in relation to other aspects of reality too. It is not shy of spreading its net widely. Personal, social, spiritual, and material reality all yield to it. Poets approach both the world and God in this way.

A particularly telling example is provided by maverick late-eighteenth-century engraver and poet William Blake. He stood historically after the pre-modern mystical era, experiencing the new world of growing enlightenment rationalism but not persuaded by it. His sense of meaning, generated primarily from visionary

29. Shakespeare, "Sonnet 18," ll. 1, 2, 9 (p. 1311).

experiences, was expressed in a riot of teasing, paradoxical, imagery and mythological narrative. The visions as he expressed them were bizarre. When he was four years old he says he saw God put his head to the window which set him screaming. Later, when he was eight or ten, as he was walking on Peckham Rye he saw "a tree filled with angels, bright angelic wings bespangling every bough like stars."[30] Could these in *any* sense be "true" visions of God? *Prima facie* it may seem unlikely to the purely rational mind. But through his poetry there are other resources for making a judgement, and these convey something very similar to the dialectic of the mystics. Through the poetically charged counterpoint of contrasting images a serious meaning is being conveyed.

He gave fullest expression to this process, and to the meaning of his visions, by creating a Tolkien-like world of mythological figures. These represent the mysterious forces and energies he was experiencing, displaying meaning through just this sort of counterpoint. He creates, for example, the figure of Urizen to describe the power of reason, and Los to describe the power of creative energy. Along with others, these characters of reason and creative energy then struggle in warfare within humanity and within the processes of creation, sometimes one assuming dominance, sometimes another, but never resolving it. They are dramatic titanic figures cast in a torrent of vivid but opaque imagery, apparently representing contrary energies of God or within God, or possibly just of human energies—the imagery is obscure. But the key feature is clear enough. In one way or another Blake is describing ultimate reality as a *co*existence of contraries. This is equally present in his shorter poems known as *Songs of Innocence and Experience*. For Blake, the texture of life, and of ultimate reality, is always this fundamental dialectic, a constant dialogue, between opposites. This is not for Blake a (pre-)Hegelian sense that these opposites move through their battle towards a resolution or synthesis, and so cease to be contrary. Instead the contraries go deeper, coexisting eternally without losing their difference. In other words, the dualities of

30. Bentley, *Blake Records*.

reason and creative energy, body and soul, all need each other *as contraries* to constitute the shape of ultimate reality.

For Blake this dialectical principle should regulate all reality, our social and political life as well as our sense of God. To refuse the dialectic and allow one pole of reality to have dominance over the other diminishes and distorts the true sense of things. In his own time this is precisely what he saw happening when scientific reason and technology began to dominate. When reason (with its affinity for uniform and universal truths) came to have primacy over creative energy (with its affinity for unique, individual, particular things) it destroyed every area of life. In the social realm these consequences could be seen in the effects of the industrial revolution where a rational appeal to efficient production had crushed and ignored individual people, and left them in appalling social conditions. His poems about the plight of young chimney sweeps in industrialized London are moving expressions of this.

But it is in relation to God, our main concern here, that Blake's approach is most germane. In his view, a failure to allow reason and creativity to coexist was particularly pernicious in religious life and belief. The result of elevating reason was to produce in his day only a remote and objectified deist God of general laws, administered oppressively through an institutionalized religion, suppressing individuality and creativity. In one poem he caricatures and lampoons this false rational image of God as an "old Nobadaddy aloft" who says "I love hanging & drawing & quartering/evry bit as well as war & slaughtering . . ."[31] This is wholly incompatible with the image of God in Jesus, where we see divine life revealed in a person who was not a slave to general laws but a creative merciful and particular interpreter of them. So the God of general laws certainly must not prevail. Equally however, Blake also warned against the opposite danger in which the meaning of God is instead reduced just to the human Jesus. God cannot be limited only to a particular relativized human embodiment. So in addition he adds: "I rest not from my great task! / To open the Eternal Worlds, to open the Immortal Eyes / Of man inwards into

31. "Let the Brothels of Paris be Opened" in Blake, *Poems and Prophecies*.

the Worlds of Thought: into Eternity / Ever expanding into the Bosom of God."[32] The key, in other words, is always to allow the vision of God its fullest possible rein. God is a reality who is not to be understood just in spirit or just in body, just in reason or just in creative energy, just in what we see as good or just in what we see in evil. Nor is God just an undifferentiated unity beyond all these. Rather, God is the reality who is constituted by them all *together*.

It is an approach which clearly resonates with the earlier pre-modern mystics. It is also notable that Blake arrived at this, like the earlier mystics, by being steeped in Scripture. He used Scripture strangely, took huge license in his rewriting of scriptural narrative in his mythologies, yet Scripture remained the launchpad. What is particularly significant, however, is not just that he draws on these earlier foundations but also still found this approach persuasive even in the midst of so-called enlightenment. At a time when the rise of science and modernity was making so much progress, before romanticism and our later disenchantments with rationalism, Blake was already realizing that a purely binary and positivist view of reason simply was not able to do full justice to reality, especially that ultimate reality we call God. It is an illustration of how persistently and pervasively this kind of mystical approach to meaning has always had purchase.

Mysticism and Postmodernity: Meaning in Play, Looking in the Gaps

The question remains, of course, whether this will always be the case. Will this rich vein of theological meaning also have significance in our current context which is no longer in the dawn of modernity like Blake but in late (or post-)modernity? It could do. After all, this is now a context in which the contested, fluid, porous, nature of both knowledge and meaning is even more widely acknowledged. So within such an open and generous zeitgeist some positive and constructive form of mystical and dialectical approach could well continue to have purchase. This has been

32. See "Jerusalem" in Blake, *Poems and Prophecies.*

borne out to some extent in both popular and formal theology, by a fairly buoyant market for so-called "mystical" teaching.

However, a context of radical skepticism about knowledge and (shared) meaning is not necessarily hospitable in a positive way. There is also the possibility that this sort of quasi-mystical theology will simply wither and die. Or it may only be able to offer a "playful" view of God. This is another very possible outcome of an era in which knowledge is generally uncertain. Where scriptural literalism, the medieval worldview, and now the modern scientific and rational worldview, have all been tried and found wanting, all we can do is play an imaginative game. We can try anything. Anything might be true. And while anything *might* mean something, it also might not. It might well mean nothing. In short, in its most radical form this playfulness with meaning (rather like the radical disruptions of "post-truth" culture) risks sterility. To mean anything and everything comes to mean nothing, just as to see through everything is to see nothing. And of course this sort of nihilism in turn might also provoke the other possible outcome of our current age which is revisionism—the return to some form of traditional authoritarianism, in theological belief as well as social realities. There is evidence of this too. Postmodernity, in short, can and probably will play host to almost anything.

Even so, there is also a more nuanced dimension to postmodernity which might offer a more positive overall outcome. This allows that both truth and meaning might still be found after all, if only and precisely *in* the gaps, impossibilities, contradictions, mysteries, which these other worldviews and explorations have bequeathed us. In other words, we may often come closest to the truth about the meaning of reality, especially ultimate reality, at points where previous explanations apparently fail. And that still means we need to *use* all the previous stories and images, even though we cannot *settle* in any of them. So this approach is by no means built just on the rejection of all that has gone before. Instead it retains some commitment to them, and ultimately still expects positive meaning from them all. It is, in other words, not just play. It is a serious business.

This holds true specifically for meanings of God. It means that if we want to describe God we will not reject but relativize and incorporate all previous categories which have cascaded through our experience and perceptions and *thereby* find new meaning both in and beyond them. So they will be included, but also transcended. It means that we will be informed by all that has already emerged in the quest for divine meaning in philosophical categories such as "transcendent spirit," "perfect rational mind," "moral demand," "unchanging ground of being," and in more concrete biblical images such as "personal presence and agent" or "the life of Christ." But it also means that we must also look through all these categories and images to see what emerges "behind" them, what they hide as well as reveal. Even then we will not see the fullness of God definitively and concretely. It is not directly grasped. But it will at least be referenced by its relation to those relativized surrounding images, and its transcendence of them. In this way the meaning of God arrives in a revelation of reality which does not just lie in any of these other human attempts to understand, but has genuinely emerged from and through them.

A picture of this way of approaching ultimate meaning (God) is provided by the way we surf the web. In his introduction to *The Postmodern God*, theologian Graham Ward described postmodern experience of the world by this analogy. In cyberspace "you can move from electric libraries in Sao Paolo, chat-lines in Florida, info sites in Sydney, data banks in Vancouver, on-line shopping in Paris, audio-visual tours with 3-d graphics of the Vatican, the White House . . . the Taj Mahal." In this experience "time and space . . . collapse . . . reality is malleable . . . permeable . . . a land of ceaseless journeying."[33] This, says Ward, is how ordinary reality now appears to us—or if not to us then to the emerging generations. He then applies this to ultimate reality, to God. The meaning of God emerges only as we, like the surfer, are "willing to lose our hold on one position and enter into many." In this late-modern world which is suspicious about all settled positions and certainties, God can only be credibly imagined in this sort of ceaseless journeying. The reality

33. Ward, *Postmodern God*, xv–xvi.

of God emerges by shifting from what is visible to what is not, and from many images and perspectives, even contrary perspectives, not just from one. Nonetheless, a substantive meaning does emerge in this way. It echoes both the earlier mystics and Blake's visionary worldview where limiting binaries are to be transcended, and that is how a fuller meaning emerges.

Does this advance us? Has it, for example, resolved the tension of those tectonic plates of contrasting images of God with which we began? The images of scriptural narratives presented God as a personal, responsive, communicating moral presence, active in history. The instincts of classical Christian Western philosophy presented God as an the *un*changing self-sufficient, perfect and absolute reality, beyond all time and change of history. Has this helped us navigate these in any new way? Perhaps not. But we could at least say that these mystical and postmodern traditions have now reframed the question so that it is no longer so pressing. It is offering a positive frame for theology within which we can more easily live with paradoxes. It is a frame which assures us that resolving them (even if we could) is actually more likely to diminish God than fully convey him. It suggests that living with apparent contradictions and ironies rather than peremptorily closing down to one dominant image will not deprive us of meaning (or truth) but may actually lead us to it.

Does this seem a threat to traditional faith? It need not. It could come as a support. After all, many core traditional images of God have themselves always required us to live with apparent contraries. That is the point. It is the biblical tradition itself which, on reflection, seems to require us to hold together in God what is both personal and transcendent, changing and unchanging. Formal doctrines, such as incarnation and Trinity, have done much the same. These images and doctrines which have pressed themselves on the church as vital ways to imagine God have always needed us to live with apparent contradiction. So the relief offered by both mystical experience and late-modern philosophy is simply that we both can live with this and should. Anything less is actually less likely to be true to God.

Admittedly it remains a challenge too. It is still potentially slippery. There is a risk that no one image or formulation of God could ever be sufficiently decisive to shape anything in our belief or our life. There is this danger that an approach which is always provisional, setting up new gaps to be explored, could imply that it is all traveling, never arriving, all just play. As indicated, that might appear so fluid it simply opens up a vacuum of destabilizing uncertainty—which dangerous fundamentalisms are bound to fill.

But this need not follow. The image of the endlessly surfing subject need not be the dominant or only image. The whole point is that there need to be other images too. So we can still choose in faith to go to some particular places more than others. After all, particular and determinate images are still *part* of the paradox, held within the restlessness of the vision, even if they cannot be the whole vision. That means we can hold to the faith (as I do) that some particularities can have peculiar authority for us within this flux. We can, for example, hold that the particularity of the Christ event *is* a unique image of the invisible God, even though still only image and not full reality. We can hold that particular dramatic biblical narratives of a personal presence and agent set some uniquely illuminating parameters, even though metaphorically expressed. In short, there are some bedrocks we can maintain.

To be sure, even with these bedrocks there is also always much to play with and play for when we imagine God. But then isn't that just how it must be if it is indeed *God* we are trying to imagine? We are always destined to be somewhat blinded by trying to look at the sun, even with all the resources handed down to us, and those still to come. Nonetheless these resources are there. Faith can and will help filter the light for those who wish to enter faith. Faith in action even more so. And I believe it remains a matter of integrity at least to try.

Conclusion

Trusting Transcendence

Nostalgia in reverse, the longing for yet another strange land
VLADIMIR NABOKOV, *MARY*

IF THERE IS ANY common golden thread to wind in from these essays it will surely be the sense of transcendence.[1] It emerges insistently as an intrinsic part of the meaning of morality, of God, and of meaning itself. As a considered concept it is arguable and contested. Nonetheless a *sense* of it is incontrovertible. Even when its metaphysical significance is denied, a sense of it remains widespread within aesthetic, moral, and spiritual experience. It is commonly encountered, as I have suggested, both as a ground and goal of morality, divinity, and meaning itself. It is also an intrinsic dimension of creative endeavor. For George Steiner a sense of transcendent reality grounds all genuine art and human attempts at communication. Art is always a response to what is beyond, not just self expression.[2] In all these ways the sense of transcendence

1. The golden thread is Blake's phrase in "Jerusalem" (Blake, *Poems and Prophecies*).
2. Cf. Steiner, *Real Presences*.

pervades experience, persisting even in secular cultures where it has been displaced from traditional theistic beliefs.[3]

But what does transcendence itself mean? Its platonic foundations in theology outlined in the previous chapter offer some contours for it. A more extensive history of its meanings in other contexts can be found elsewhere.[4] Broadly speaking it refers to a dimension of reality which lies beyond the limits of our current categories of knowing, being and speaking. While it may include them in some way it also radically differs. So whereas our finitude appears to impose absolute limits to our knowing and being, the sense of transcendence suggests these boundaries are not as absolute as they appear to be. Under certain conditions they are, or become, porous, dispensable, or surmountable. Like a horizon, they mark only *apparent* limits, not ultimate limits.

Within this broad understanding of transcendence there are radical and less radical interpretations, "external" and "internal" notions of transcendence.[5] The most radical meanings conceive transcendence as a wholly different register of reality. It is conceived it as truly *sui generis*, a different order of being altogether from anything currently known to which language and experience can only point never directly describe or engage.[6] Less radical meanings conceive the difference within the same order of being, allowing more direct comparison with what is already known.[7]

3. Charles Taylor has mapped this extensively and persuasively in his major work *Secular Age*.

4. Taylor, *Secular Age*. Taylor's work deals with it largely from the point of view of social philosophy. Within theology notable examples are Tanner, *God and Creation in Christian Theology*; Placher, *Domestication of Transcendence*.

5. Nussbaum, *Love's Knowledge*. Nussbaum is wary of finding meaning in any notion of transcendence so outside the ordinary human experience of successiveness that it contradicts it, so prefers to think of a capacity to transcend linear time as an "internal" transcendence.

6. Radical transcendence can be traced in Western philosophy and religion back to platonic and mystical traditions, the "ineffable One" of Plotinus, Eckhart, and more existential traditions of Kierkegaard and Karl Jaspers. It also has a counterpart in late modern ethical reflection, e.g., in Levinas.

7. In medieval philosophy this is usually associated with Duns Scotus. He postulated a "shared" property of being between God and creaturely reality.

The former is something like the transcendence of a dreamer to his dream, an author to the characters of her plot, or of three-dimensional space to a two-dimensional drawing. The latter is more like the transcendence we exercise through our minds when revisiting our memories, or exploring the structures of the universe intellectually just from a stationary armchair.

These analogies are not precise. Nor are they immune to critique. A common complaint about the most radical notions of transcendence is simply that they are nonsensical.[8] Anything *wholly* other is by definition wholly unthinkable and unspeakable. If it "exists" at all it exists in such a different way that it is entirely meaningless to us. But this allows no latitude or nuance in the terms. Radical otherness need not necessarily mean the wholly other in every respect. What lies wholly beyond us in some fundamental aspect may have some relation to it in another aspect. And this means that thought and language derived from our current existence can at least *point* to what is radically beyond itself, as a signpost in one landscape can point to a wholly unseen reality over the horizon (while itself wholly embedded in its own side). Analogy, which employs both likeness and unlikeness, is a linguistic template for communicating this sort of meaning.

Where can we find this sense of radical transcendence? Beyond the generalities of spirituality, art, and creativity, can we be more specific? The most obvious sites are those which these essays have been exploring. It is found in the presenting experiences and internal logic of both morality and traditional theology. It certainly has to apply when we are thinking of an infinite *God*.[9] But it is not special pleading in theology. It routinely impinges on us, for example, simply in the sense of perfection we have about many things, although they do not actually display perfection. The idea of perfection haunts us even though perfection itself lies over the horizon. So its absence in experience is not an absolute barrier to

8. Cf. Caputo, "God Is Wholly Other."

9. This is a major part of the previous chapter. I have also argued this in more detail elsewhere. See White, "Future of Theology," and White, *Purpose and Providence.*

conceiving it. Instead, like an echo or shadow the absence has left an imprint which thought can at least follow like a signpost. This holds true for almost everything we find important in life. With love, beauty, being itself, we may never have experienced their ultimacy and perfection but we can and do still imagine it may exist "somewhere," and that is precisely because of this imprint of it which we *do* have in our experience. Augustine memorably explored this sense in his *Confessions*, reflecting on the experiences of learning, beauty, and memory. He finds in these experiences a sense of something whose perfection is truly beyond the self, even as he finds it signaled within the self.

In a very different register of thought, twentieth-century German philosopher Karl Jaspers also sensed transcendence through the experience of tragedy. Tragedy is inevitable within the structures of reality we inhabit. It is a world where values are bound to collide, idealism will be frustrated and suffering will occur. And it is inevitable because of our limits and finitude not just because of wilful human fault. *But* why then, in the face of tragedy, are we still haunted by a persistent sense of failure and a guilt which is often a "guiltless" guilt? Why are we still hounded by a persistent (and impossible) sense of moral imperative to surmount this inevitable tragedy? Where does this perfectionism come from? Jaspers faced these issues *in extremis* in the aftermath of the Second World War in Germany as a psychiatrist, but found no adequate answer just in psychological terms. For him it required philosophically reframing reality as a whole to account for it. Only if there is a transcendent dimension beyond tragedy can our profound protest against tragedy make any sense. Only an objective reality of transcendence provides an origin for the perfectionist demand which keeps echoing in us without regard to our actual limitations.[10]

Finally, transcendence is also found in the experience of a particular kind of yearning. There is a yearning, not uncommon, which has an irresistible gravitational pull on us even though it has no clear object. Its object may touch on love, beauty, joy. It may include truth and justice. But these alone fail to do justice to

---

10. Jaspers, *Tragedy Is Not Enough.*

the full density of the experience. "Home" is possibly the closest we shall get to identifying it, a reality we may think we know but do not yet fully inhabit and still yearn for. Within this experience, the yearning itself, not just its object, is also elusive. *Sehnsucht* may be its most apt linguistic form: "thoughts and feelings about life that are unfinished or imperfect, paired with a yearning for ideal alternative experiences."[11] It is an unspecified, unfulfilled desire for an order of being or *modus vivendi* which is itself beyond specifying and beyond our current experience, while also registering profoundly within us. It is, in C. S. Lewis's description, the transcendence of a "far country," always beyond us even though sensed within us. He evokes it like this:

> In speaking of this desire for our own far off country, which we find in ourselves even now, I feel a certain shyness. I am almost committing an indecency. I am trying to rip open the inconsolable secret in each one of you—the secret which hurts so much that you take your revenge on it by calling it names like Nostalgia and Romanticism and Adolescence. . . . . the secret we cannot hide and cannot tell, though we desire to do both. We cannot tell it because it is a desire for something that has never actually appeared in our experience. We cannot hide it because our experience is constantly suggesting it, and we betray ourselves like lovers at the mention of a name. Our commonest expedient is to call it beauty and behave as if that had settled the matter. Wordsworth's expedient was to identify it with certain moments in his own past. . . . These things—the beauty, the memory of our own past— are good images of what we really desire; but . . . .they are not the thing itself; they are only the scent of a flower we have not found, the echo of a tune we have not heard, news from a country we have never visited.[12]

All these expressions of transcendence help fill out its meaning. They are selective, always open to different interpretation, and contestable in many ways. But they are at least sufficient to give

11. Kotter-Grühn et al., "What Is It?"
12. Lewis, "Weight of Glory"

some indication why, however hard to conceptualize, transcendence remains such a pervasive compelling notion. It convinces because it refers to a reality beyond our current experience whose signs are also inextricably enfolded within experience. It compels because it offers a reason for why we have experiences which grip us. It is why, whenever we "stick our finger into existence" (Kierkegaard's phrase,)[13] whether it currently seems thick or thin, dense with meaning or disconcertingly light, existence still has such a strange hold on us. In short, transcendence is what grounds all our own more tenuous and fickle created meanings, and makes things *matter*. It is what tells us that they are not all just contingent and transitory but also have an ultimate ground and destiny.

Can we trust it? I believe we can. As the word "trust" implies, all this must ultimately be an article of faith. But this faith is well grounded, as I hope to have shown. Experience and reflection alike point to it as signs point over a horizon. They show, even though they cannot make us fully see, that there really is a meaning to morality, to God, and to meaning itself.

---

13. Kierkegaard, *Repetition*.

Bibliography

Affolter, Jacob. "Human Nature as God's Purpose." *Religious Studies* 43 (2007) 443–55.

Auerbach, Eric. *Mimesis: The Representation of Reality in Western Literature.* Princeton: Princeton University Press, 1953/2003

Barnes, Julian. *The Sense of an Ending.* London: Jonathan Cape, 2011.

Barth, Karl. *Church Dogmatics* III/3. Edinburgh: T. & T. Clark, 1976.

Bauman, Zygmunt. *Liquid Modernity.* Cambridge: Polity, 2000.

Beer, Gillian. *Darwin's Plots.* Cambridge: Cambridge University Press, 2000.

Bentley, G. E. *Blake Records.* New Haven, CT: Yale University Press, 2004.

Berger, Peter. *A Rumour of Angels.* London: Penguin, 1969.

Blake, William. *Poems and Prophecies.* London: Dent Dutton, 1970.

Bonhoeffer, Dietrich. *Letters and Papers from Prison.* London: SCM, 1967.

Burgess, Bev. *Executive Engagement Strategies.* Harvard Business Review. London: Kogan Page, 2020.

Butler, Judith. "Jacques Derrida." In *The Meaningless of Meaning*, 111–16. London: LRB, 2020.

Caputo, John D. "God Is Wholly Other—Almost: 'Différance' and the Hyperbolic Alterity of God." In *The Otherness of God*, edited by Orrin Summerell, 190–205. Charlottesville: University of Virginia Press, 1998.

Conant, James, and Sebastian Sunday, eds. *Wittgenstein on Philosophy, Objectivity, and Meaning.* Cambridge: Cambridge University Press, 2019.

Critchley, Simon. *Infinitely Demanding.* London: Verso, 2007.

Cupitt, Don. *Taking Leave of God.* London: SCM, 2001.

Demos Report. *Entrepreneurship and the Wired Life.* London: Demos, 2000

Eliot, George. *Middlemarch.* London: Penguin, 1973.

Eliot, T.S. *Four Quartets.* London: Faber and Faber, 1944.

Farley, Margaret. *Personal Commitments.* San Francisco: Harper & Row, 1990.

Ferry, Luc. *Man Made God: The Meaning of Life.* Translated by David Pellauer. Chicago: University of Chicago, 2002.

Bibliography

Foot, Philippa. *Natural Goodness.* Oxford: Clarendon, 2001.

Giddens, Anthony. *The Consequences of Modernity.* Cambridge: Polity, 1990.

———. *Modernity and Self-Identity.* Cambridge: Polity, 1991.

Hardy, Thomas. *Tess of the d'Urbervilles.* Oxford: Oxford University Press, 1983.

Held, David, and John B. Thompson, eds. *Social Theory of Modern Societies: Anthony Giddens and His Critics.* Cambridge: Cambridge University Press, 2009.

Hemingway, Ernest. *For Whom the Bell Tolls.* London: Penguin, 1994.

Heriot, Peter, and Carol Pemberton. *New Deals. The Revolution in Managerial Careers.* Chichester: John Wiley & Sons, 1995.

Jaspers, Karl. *Tragedy Is Not Enough.* Boston: Beacon, 1952.

Kermode, Frank. "Waiting for the End." In *Apocalypse Theory and the End of the World,* edited by Malcolm Bull, 250–63. Oxford: Blackwell, 1995.

Kershaw, Ian. "Working Towards the Führer: Reflections on the Nature of the Hitler." In *The Third Reich,* edited by Christian Leitz, 231–52. London: Blackwell, 1999.

Kierkegaard, Søren. *Repetition and Philosophical Crumbs.* Oxford: Oxford University Press, 2009.

Kotter-Grühn, D., et al. "What Is It We Are Longing For? Psychological and Demographic Factors Influencing the Contents of Sehnsucht (Life Longings)." *Journal of Research in Personality* 43 (2009) 428–37.

Kundera, Milan. *The Unbearable Lightness of Being.* London: Faber & Faber, 1985.

Lewis, C. S. "The Weight of Glory." In *Screwtape Proposes a Toast,* 97–98. London: Fontana, 1965.

Lipsey, Roger. *Hammarskjöld: A Life.* Ann Arbor, MI: University of Michigan Press, 2013.

MacIntyre, Alasdair. *After Virtue.* London: Duckworth, 1985.

Mane, Kate. "The Nice and the Good." *Times Literary Supplement,* February 11, 2022.

Marcel, Gabriel. *Being and Having.* Westminster: Dacre, 1949.

———. *Creative Fidelity.* New York: Farrar, Straus, 1964.

McGrath, Alister. *Faith and the Creeds.* London: SPCK, 2013.

Niebuhr, H. Richard. *Radical Monotheism and Western Culture.* London: Faber, 1961.

———. *The Responsible Self.* New York: Harper & Row, 1963.

Nussbaum, Martha. *Love's Knowledge. Essays on Philosophy and Literature.* Oxford: Oxford University Press, 1990.

Placher, William. *The Domestication of Transcendence.* Louisville, KY: Westminster John Knox, 1996.

Pseudo-Dionysius. "The Mystical Theology." In *Pseudo-Dionysius: The Complete Works,* 133–41. New York: Paulist, 1987.

Pullman, Philip. "God and Dust." In *Daemon Voices. Essays in Storytelling,* 423–40. Oxford: David Fickling, 2017.

————. "Poco a Poco." In *Daemon Voices. Essays in Storytelling*, 205–38. Oxford: David Fickling, 2017.

Royce, Josiah. *The Philosophy of Loyalty*. New York: Macmillan, 1908.

Shakespeare, William. "Sonnet 18." In *The Complete Works of William Shakespeare*, edited by Peter Alexander, 1311. London: Collins, 1964.

Stacey, Judith. *Brave New Families*. New York: Basic, 1990.

Steiner, George. *Real Presences*. London: Faber & Faber, 1989.

Strawson, Galen. *Things That Bother Me*. New York: New York Review Books, 2018.

Tanner, Kathryn. *God and Creation in Christian Theology: Tyranny or Empowerment*. Oxford: Blackwell, 1988.

Taylor, Charles. *A Secular Age*. Cambridge: Harvard University Press, 2007.

Taylor, John V. *The Go-Between God*. London: SCM, 1972.

Turner, Denys. *The Darkness of God: Negativity in Christian Mysticism*. Cambridge: Cambridge University Press, 1995.

Ward, Graham, ed. *The Postmodern God*. Oxford: Blackwell, 1997.

Ward, Keith. *God: A Guide for the Perplexed*. Oxford: Oneworld, 2002.

White, Vernon. "The Future of Theology." In *Calling Time. Religion and Change at the Turn of the Millennium*, edited by Martyn Percy, 205–20. Sheffield: Sheffield Academic, 2000.

————. "Idealism and Compromise." In *The Moral Heart of Public Service*, edited by Claire Foster-Gilbert, 123–71. London: Jessica Kingsley, 2015.

————. *Identity*. London: SCM, 2002.

————. *Purpose and Providence. Taking Soundings in Western Thought, Literature and Theology*. London: T. & T. Clark, 2018.

Wright, N. T. *Paul and the Faithfulness of God*. London: SPCK, 2013.

Yong, Amos. "Divining 'Divine Action' in Theology-and-Science: A Review Essay." *Zygon* 43 (2008) 191–200.

Young, Frances. *Face to Face: A Narrative Essay in the Theology of Suffering*. Edinburgh: T. & T. Clark, 1991.

Index of Names

Affolter, Jacob, 16n8, 22n16
Aquinas, Thomas, 82n13
Auerbach, Eric, 68,70
Augustine, Saint, 92

Barnes, Julian, 13n3, 24–25
Barth, Karl, 26n21
Bauman, Zygmunt, 48
Beer, Gillian, 21n14
Benedict, Saint, 50n14
Bentley, G. F. 98
Berger, Peter, 20n13
Blake, William, 97–100, 105
Bonhoeffer, Dietrich, 86
Buber, Martin, 73
Butler, Judith, 25

Caputo, John, 107n8
Christ, Jesus, 60, 65–66, 69, 72, 77, 84
Clement of Alexandria, 92
Conant, James, 8n2
Critchley, Simon, 23, 37–38, 39, 44, 76
Cupitt, Don, 96

Derrida, Jacques, 25, 26
Deutsch, Karl, 46

Duns Scotus, John, 106n7

Eckhart, Meister, 96, 106n6
Eliot, George, 30–31
Eliot, T. S., 87

Farley, Margaret, 59n23
Ferry, Luc, 8n1, 14
Foot, Philippa, 16
Forster, E. M. 7

Giddens, Anthony, 52–53

Hardy, Thomas, 18–19
Hammarskjöld Dag, 45n8, 46
Held, David, 52n18
Hemingway, Ernest, 40
Heraclitus, 59
Hitler, Adolf, 77, 86
Homer, 68

James, William, 16n7
Jaspers, Karl, 42n7, 46n10, 106n6, 108
John, Saint, 92

Kant, Immanuel, 28, 38, 61, 75
Kermode, Frank, 49

115

Index of Names

Kershaw, Ian, 77n11
Kierkegaard, Søren, 106n6, 110
Kotter-Grühn, D., 108n11
Kundera, Milan, 51n16

Lewis, C. S., 108
Lipsey, Roger, 45
Luther, Martin, 37

MacDonald, George, 1
MacIntyre, Alasdair, 50n14
Marcel, Gabriel, 52
McGrath, Alister, 90n20
Moses, 66, 69, 77

Nabokov, Vladimir, 105
Niebuhr, H. Richard, 60n25
Nussbaum, Martha, 106n5

Ogden, C. K., 7
Origen, 92

Parmenides, 59
Paul, Saint, 69, 92
Pemberton, Carole, 57n20
Placher, William, 87n16
Plato, 38, 59, 81, 83, 92
Philo, 92
Plotinus, 106n6
Pseudo-Dionysius, 93–94
Pullman, Philip, 18–19, 21

Richards, I. A., 7
Royce, Josiah, 51, 60

Sayers, Dorothy, 90
Shakespeare, William, 38, 97
Stacey, Judith, 55n19
Steiner, George, 105
Strawson, Galen, 14n5
Sunday, Sebastian, 8n2

Tanner, Kathryn, 106n4
Taylor, Charles, 23, 106n3,n4
Taylor, John V., 74n8
Tennyson, Alfred, 62
Thompson, John B., 52n18
Turner, Denys, 96n28

Ward, Graham, 102
Ward, Keith, 64–65
White, Vernon, 13n3, 15n6, 41n5, 47, 107n9
Wittgenstein, Ludwig, 8n2, 94
Wright, N. T., 60n25

Yong, Amos, 89n19
Young, Frances, 88, 89n18

Milton Keynes UK
Ingram Content Group UK Ltd.
UKHW040739040823
426323UK00004B/136

9 781666 764864